DOUBLE TAKE!

("Unholy" insights on the "holy" institutions
of formal education, religion, marriage,
social work, etc.)

Margarita Ventenilla-Hamada

(Author of *School Mythtakes*)

New Day Publishers
Quezon City
1991

EXCLUSIVE DISTRIBUTORS:
THE CELLAR BOOK SHOP
18090 WYOMING
DETROIT, MICH. 48221
U.S.A.

Cover Design: JOHN SIBAL

ISBN 971-10-0432-1

To my children—

Anthony, Ulysses and Farrah,

the living reasons behind all my achievements

Acknowledgment

Sincerest thanks to Thaddy Mapula,

for his indispensable know-how on computers

and word-processing,

and his patience in imparting it to me.

Foreword

Seldom do we encounter any piece of literature or prose that is not in the very least bowdlerized, stripped of essences and beclouded by the inherent cognitive presuppositions and linguistic blinders of editors.

Double Take!, a very personal book on a variety of subjects, precisely embodies the exercise of intellectual liberty, a trait that has somehow been lost in the minds of many writers now, particularly those engaged in hagiography or those who make giants out of runts, saints out of devils and demigods out of lesser mortals.

As a writer myself, I have rarely seen works of philosophical and epistemological import that attempt to really go down to the roots of all heretofore existing societal myths, ideological truisms and tautological formulations. *Double Take!* is precisely one such attempt, not only from the vantage point of the author's trove of intellectual gems but also from her definitive but seemingly iconoclastic ideological bent.

Witness the long reflection on the role of education as a process and as a way of life, not as a hierarchic framework but as a liberating experience that each individual must pass through if enlightenment were to be attained.

The reader can find gems in the discussion on the real worth of money, the impact of science, the proper place of religion and the ideological systems that have so far encrusted liberating human consciousness with barnacles of reactionary fixity. The author, like a sudden storm after a long drought, attacks the dormant seeds with violence at first, then later on with grace, like a mother's caress.

The honesty that literally straddles all this book's pages adds more impact on the message that the author wishes to impart: the individual as the repository of values, nay of virtues, that need to be sired, nurtured and later on given birth through a period of deliberate intellectual and spiritual labor. All religions or belief systems have failed to nurture the near perfect man, conscious of being, aware of duty, knowledgeable about his or her role in society and the cosmic unity. The author's project, if we may venture to add, is to set an entirely new appreciation of all heretofore exiting biases and prejudices, particularly in the structures, social or cognitive, that bind us with nature and with ourselves.

It is not only in achieving that we are made rich; it is also in feeling empty or lacking that we strive to learn more, gain insights and strive to pass through the impediments that society have arbitrarily set up to chain man and prevent his ascent to the limits of intellectual and spiritual growth. There is no hard and fast rule in reaching enlightenment as there is no law governing the exercise of the inherent capabilities of the human being is attaining his or her intellectual nirvana.

The author draws from a wealth of intellectual sources to buttress her contention about the miseducation we have all gone through. For an educator to say this without rancor is itself incredible. For her to batter the ossified thinking and the fossilized values attached to formalistic education is amazing, a contribution no less to the current debate on the educational system and the ideological axioms that have so far made education unwieldy and uncaring of its objects.

Yet, our interest is drawn to the fact that the author makes no bones about her interest in destroying the very cul-de-sac that has so far produced graduates without direction, led by the blind and employed by the uncaring. We can all agree that education in this country is treading dangerous grounds as idiotization, rather than enlightenment, has been given top priority, with students and graduates alike looking like automatons what with their unscrupulous proclivity to rote memory, aversion to critical thinking and hatred of real knowledge to change the world and make man one with himself and nature.

Heretofore, all scholarship has centered on merely prettifying or fulminating against perceived social anomalies or historical incongruities, not with the structure of scholarship and the systems of rational or irrational conventions that have warped the exercise and propagation of correct values and ideas.

Double Take! is an essay into the possibility of changing timeworn epistemological biases with the end in view of rigorously subjecting ideological in the crucible of intellectual, practical and spiritual practice. If we may use the term *praxis* here, we must use education as both theory and practice, the sensual and the vicarious, unstructured but systematic, objective as well as subjective and everywhere impinging on the higher idea of making knowledge serve its object without in any way disturbing the dialectical relationship between knowledge and its various epiphenomena, be they science or the arts.

It comes as no surprise that the author also dwelt on the anecdotal in much of the work. A very personal book finds merit only when it uses life as a consistent background, a spring from which to draw nuggets of experience and, to say the most, real unadulterated knowledge. Her struggle in marriage betrays her uncanny ability to reiterate the experiential back to the level of the ideological, not in a way ceding to platitudes what should rightfully be stressed, in bold relief yet, in lcud, unequivocal terms.

This book may actually be searching for an audience since no book hereabouts creates an audience purely on the depth of its prognostications or the accuracy of its prosaic perorations. Inexorably, her prudent essaying of the ideological problems show in clear terms how her pristine outlook has not been infiltrated by the illusions provided by false knowledge. Many authors have not been able to combat the dire effects of ideological baggage they have harbored; the author in this instance has simply dismissed the luggage as ineffectual and eventually false and must be seen as such and treated with scorn even as it must be turned back against itself. Ideologies and false knowledge exist only when society and man could not surpass or leap beyond what is.

We should be glad that we have had the chance to savor the fine intellectual dish that Ms. Margarita Ventenilla Hamada has offered us. It might yet be a fine addition to the growing literature on holistic education for the whole man, a virtual encyclopedia of old ideas turned upside down to give birth to new significant maxims. I trust that any reader would find mere reading this book as inadequate; it must be discussed and discussed thoroughly to make it serve its real purpose.

MIRIAM DEFENSOR SANTIAGO
May 9, 1990

Contents

Part One

FORMAL EDUCATION

*". . . that is ever the difference
between the wise and the unwise;
the latter wonders at what is unusual,
the wise man wonders at the usual."*

—Ralph Waldo Emerson

1

The True Mark of an Educated Person

WELLESLEY COLLEGE, one of the seven top colleges for women in the United States, has made its aim very clear: it does not aim to turn out doctors, scientists, prime ministers, senators or justices, although its alumnae may eventually end up as any one or several of these. Its president, addressing the parents of the freshmen last year, said that its only aim is to "turn out women who can communicate well." A very simple aim. But a very profound one. And, if examined more closely, it is the only aim that is rational and good. For communicating well is the hallmark of an educated person. What use is an academic title or a government position if you cannot give definite shape to a thought that is imprisoned in you and thereby imprisons you? When you lose, instead of gain, a value because you cannot unlock the chains with the right word and style? When you cannot command the respect your position should entitle you to because your grammar and syntax fit the wilderness better than the civilization represented by your chair?

If you were a surgeon and you had to explain to your prospective patient certain procedures of the operation you will perform in bastardized grammar, do you think you will gain that patient's confidence so that he will entrust his life in your hands? Incoherence is incompetence. And it never pays. It should never be excused, especially in professions that are called "talkative professions" like teaching, law, and the ministry. Poor communicators have no business calling themselves teachers or lawyers or judges and practising such professions, even if sanctioned by the Department of Education that they can do so. They won't stay long as such, anyway, without the help of a politician, in exchange for a big favor.

Mastery of communication skills, especially written communication, is mastery over stagnation. It is true that knowledge is the key to progress, but it is "useless unless you know how to communicate it—in writing," emphasized David Ogilvy. His position as president of his own ad agency, OGILVY & MATHER, is proof that "the better you write,

3

the higher you go. People who think well, write well!" he declared.

Therefore, to produce not academicians or statesmen or scientists, but educated people—people who can communicate well—must be the aim of all our schools, because good communicators can easily become anyone they choose to be, and whether they choose to be a doctor, a lawyer, a scientist, a technologist, a nurse, or a teacher, they will easily find themselves at the top of their chosen career. On the other hand, poor communicators usually end up nowhere, or if anywhere, it would be at the bottom of the heap, and remain there, regardless of their university degrees. Schools must concentrate on this one aim and must not be tempted to veer directions towards being a "science school," emphasizing content in science subjects instead of skills in communication. In other words, first things first. The dress first, before the trimming. Schools can produce writers and communicators if they don't smother students with subjects required by the NCEE, like Science and Advanced Math. A written paragraph is a better measure of intellect than a booklet of machine-scored exams like the NCEE because writing comes, says Emerson, "from greater depth and scope of thought."

Do you communicate well, orally or in writing? Then you are an educated person, no matter if you have a degree to validate your being so or not. Do you stammer and mix up your he and she and your tenses? Do you say "mean" when you should say "men"? Then you are not educated, merely schooled. You are not yet free to reach your star, however much scientific knowledge your mind holds or how many intricate mathematical formulae you have memorized. You have to learn the rudiments of the most basic skills in literacy—communication skills.

Communication skills can be learned by doing two things constantly: reading and writing. Read books that are not required by your school, but those which your natural interest leads you to. "A man ought to read just as inclination leads him; for what he reads as a task will do him little good," Samuel Johnson cautions us with this wise observation. Keep a journal and write down your thoughts and feelings every day. Write letters. Re-read your favorite books. Discuss ideas with people whose ideas you admire. Learn at least five new words a day. And remember to have fun at it. You learn best when you are not too serious and earnest. "Many times we will get more and better ideas in two hours of creative loafing than in eight hours at a desk," enunciates Wilfred Peterson. Bertrand Russell says the same thing: "It is only in a spirit of free inquiry that desirable learning can take place." Work is something you have to do, where you have to be serious and earnest.

Play is something you want to do, with no trace of seriousness at all. Yet, writes Robert Frost, America's beloved poet:

> Only when love and need are one,
> And the work is play for mortal stakes,
> Is the deed ever truly done,
> For Heaven and the future's sakes.

Your reward? Not cum laude honors but something substantially better: a well-earned position in life and one that is well-deserved, too, without the help of any politician. Plus . . . integrity or wholeness that only an educated person is privileged to hold and keep. For, as articulated for us by my favorite philosopher, Ralph Waldo Emerson, "All men live by truth and stand in need of expression . . . the man is only half himself. The other half his expression."

Communication, because it liberates and integrates, is ultimately power—that power within that beats all powers without. Let our schools lay the foundation for this paramount skill. And if they don't or won't, do it yourself, no matter how old you are. You can do it. Then, you can indeed zoom up to that star and hitch your wagon to it.

2

The Hidden Rewards of Journal Writing

(Editorial, The Magic Pencil, *1988 issue)*

IN HARVENT SCHOOL, our pupils do something every day that children from other schools do not do: they spend an hour each day writing in their journals. Every Friday, teachers select a journal entry or two, write the entry on the board en toto without the writer's name, to be corrected by the group. Journal writing is an important activity that polishes pupils' writing skills—their spelling and grammar and the mechanics of good writing. Very few know the hidden concomitants of this activity. Journal writing does not only develop the pupils' grammar, but more important, it develops their higher mental processes: choosing, observing, comparing, summarizing, imagining, criticizing, synthesizing, analyzing, defining, inquiring, creating and explaining.

As founder/director of Harvent School, I have kept in mind the sad fact that the schools I had attended as a child failed to give me exercises in the above mental processes. The only mental process they gave us too much drill on happens to belong to the lowest rung among all mental processes—memorization of facts on pain of failure. As a result, my classmates and I found it difficult after graduation to cope with reality outside school because reality does not demand information but skills in thinking and strategizing. Some of us therefore got lost in our careers, some of us took the wrong directions, some of us chose the wrong spouses, some of us keep following the crowd until now. Most are stumped by economic difficulties. Many can hardly realize even a few of the many rose-colored dreams we had when we were schoolgirls. I know at least two intelligent classmates in high school who resorted to obscene talents just to get ahead in life—selling themselves to the same rich man, all because their degrees could not even buy them a car or land them a prestigious position. Their formal schooling somehow undercut their power within, and so they resorted to the power without. Knowing the worst of what formal schools can do, it is difficult to contain

6

within one's breast a savage rage.

I made my anger and resentment work positively for me and my children and their schoolmates by establishing Harvent School. It is the only school that does not teach information. It only teaches SKILLS in the basics and polishes these with merciless drills and develops pupils' higher mental processes so that they can cope with reality outside school. It does not teach science the way I was taught during my school days.

However, my work is being made difficult by parents who cannot see the beautiful results and their significance. But I can hardly blame them for it is always difficult, nay, impossible, to see the abstract. And SKILLS are abstract. MENTAL PROCESSES are abstract. They cannot be seen by the naked eye, especially when the eye does not seek to see beyond the surface. On the surface, pupils from other schools who are trained to copy and memorize information appear to be better educated than my pupils in Harvent School because data can be seen. Information is asked for by entrance exams, whose validity and importance are questionable, but are still being used. And entrance exams are part of this educational system of which Harvent School is not a part. No entrance exam asks pupils to demonstrate their analytical skills or their imaginativeness or their ability to inquire into facts. In fact, schools are afraid of pupils who think because they are so afraid to be challenged and exposed for their wrong values and misdirections. So they admit pupils whose mental processes have been left undeveloped. They're safer with them that way. Thinkers? Who cares for that bunch of troublemakers—who'll cry for reforms and put them out of their business? Only a few of us care. We care because we owe our progress to thinkers, no matter how bloody the road to progress is. And it is only the resistance of these lovers of the status quo which accounts for the bloodshed. We need thinkers to get us out of our present problems. We need thinkers so that we can realize our dreams with our integrity still intact. We need thinkers to direct us to a better way of life.

Harvent School is proud to show the results of its work towards creating thinkers. Here, in these pages of *The Magic Pencil*, pupils as young as four give new insights on life in this old world. Perhaps, it is not premature for us to believe that this world is headed towards peace and progress because of these young thinkers we produce every year. A difficult job, but nevertheless a good one, because its rewards come in terms of a brighter future for all of us—rewards visible only to the few of us who can see the invisible.

3

Literacy in English Is Our Business

*(Closing remarks on Harvent School's Achievers' Day,
25 March 1990)*

MY DEAR ACHIEVERS, their proud parents and grandparents, Mr. PTA president and members of the Board, Miss Carla Corona and her mother, Mrs. Tina Corona, ladies and gentlemen:

If you examine the contents of the leading daily newspapers carefully, you will not fail to notice that there are several advertisements running along this same line: Improve your English. Seminars and Dale Carnegie crash courses are offered to students and professionals in Better Business Letter Writing and Speech Power and Personality Development. In bookstores, most of the books classified under self-help books are mostly about Correct English, Vocabulary Building and Word Power, and Developing Self-confidence. These courses and books are expensive. A two-week speech course costs P1,200. Yet, reservations are made in advance because of the heavy enrollment. The need for people who can communicate well in English, both orally and in writing, is so great that these businesses have earned millions for their owners. Books on choosing the right word and improving one's vocabulary cost between P300 to P500 each. And yet they are snapped up as fast as they are displayed on the shelves.

The message of this scenario is sharp and clear: our schools are not teaching English very well, despite the fact that our country has grown with the times, despite the fact that our national boundaries have extended themselves to embrace the whole English-speaking world. Ever since the incongruous wave of nationalism has hit our shores and Filipino has become the medium of instruction, ever since the elementary and the high schools decided to detract precious hours from their curricula in favor of science and social studies, parents have become saddled with a new expense—the high cost of these Speech and

8

Personality Development courses their children have to attend to learn good English they could not otherwise learn in their regular schools.

It is with urgent concern that I bring this matter to your attention, so you will see more easily my purpose in staying in Lingayen and running Harvent School. I have made literacy in English my business so that the parents of my pupils need not run into the high cost of enrolling their children in Manila schools for them to speak and write English very well.

I could easily have stayed in Manila or gone off to New York after college, but I did not. I decided to share my gift for communication with you. Because of Harvent School's emphasis on English communication and personality development which is a direct result of its non-graded method, I am confident that our community will receive added assets each year in the persons of my alumni. They, like Carla Corona, can better define their goals in life with these skills, with these assets, and can more easily steer society towards peace and progress. Without communication skills and the confidence these skills inevitably bring to their personality, they would be sorely handicapped in this modern global society we are now members of.

My sincere thanks to the members of my staff who, like me, decided to stay in the province and help me deliver literacy in English and, at the same time, make our pupils aware of the beauty of one's town and country; to my dear college friend, Tina Roco Corona, who has watched me work at my ideals with approval and pride, and for having come all the way from Manila to grace our gala affair today; to her daughter, Carla, who has shown the world and us that being proficient in English has added to, and not detracted from, the glory of her Filipino heritage, and to you, dear parents, for having entrusted your children's education in my hands, and for having allowed me to draw forth bright tomorrows for all of us from their total development.

Thank you and good afternoon to all.

4

Help! Procrustes Is Here!

(*Published in* Parents Magazine,
Vol. 2, No. 3, June-July 1989 issue)

BELIEVE IT OR NOT, there's such a thing as mass insanity or mass stupidity, and it seems that this malady strikes a civilization when it reaches its peak. This malady flourishes for hundreds of years before its barbarity is finally exposed and stamped out.

India, at the height of its splendor, espoused the criminally stupid tradition of suttee. Widows immolated themselves in the funeral pyre of their husbands, showing the public that their love for the deceased surpassed their love of self and their love for and responsibility to their children whom they wilfully, premeditatedly left behind as orphans in their cruel society. It was suicide sanctioned and sanctified. Suttees were "canonized" as saints! Widows who refused to be suttees because they were rational and therefore had no need to impress anyone at the cost of their own lives and their children's well-being were ostracized and cursed. It was the reign of irrationality and therefore of terror. Of values upside down: valuing the dead more than the living. Burning the most valuable and only sacred thing in the world—one's life, for something as worthless as the applause of madmen. Public approval for abandoning one's own children and abdication of the right to think. Public censure for responsibility and rationality.

China, at its zenith, also developed a malady—a mania for deformity in the form of a tradition or custom which was just as barbarous and criminally stupid as the suttee—binding girls' feet. Those highly civilized Chinese considered what was natural as shameful, and banded together to destroy nature's design of what women's feet should look like. They bound their infant daughters' feet and encased them in heavy iron shoes, without anesthesia, ignoring the physical pain and the consequent loss of mobility which could prove fatal in case of emergencies such as fire. Girls who refused to submit to this protracted torture were called "peasants" and lost all chances of marrying into the nobility. Those who submitted were rewarded with social distinction and therefore with a good marriage—but with a permanent, irreversible handicap.

And now, the developed countries—in Europe, USA, Japan, Canada, Australia—are stricken with Procrustes' syndrome. (Procrustes was a madman in Greek mythology who invited his guests to sleep on his special bed. He then cut off their feet or heads if they were longer than the bed, and stretched them if they were shorter until their sinews snapped from their sockets.) The educators of these nations have conspired against the youth by inventing a special machinery called formal schooling. The school they have designed is more barbarous than the Indian or Chinese customs, and bloodier/deadlier than Procrustes' bed, for it deliberately deforms the mind and personality of children—not just their feet or bodies, to fit them to a special bed called "prescribed curriculum." The school, like primitive man, worships freaks and seeks to produce what nature did not give them. It legalizes the changing of what is natural and good. Primitive man exerted effort and spent time to change nature's design for art's sake. Thus he flattened and elongated his skull by the painful process of sandwiching his head between two boards pressed together. (A trip to the Ayala Museum will illuminate my point better.) He filed his teeth and blackened them. He tattooed his body. He punctured his nose and slipped a bone through it. All without anesthesia. Educators in these highly civilized nations do the same barbarity with the same zeal, but not even for art's sake—but just to express the symptoms of this mental disease that has gripped them. Pupils who enter school with a definite shape—i.e., they have natural inclinations and individual differences, emerge from it totally altered. They are uniformly well-rounded and bloated with trivia. They are compelled to study science, math, history, economics, music and art all at once, from teachers who are not scientists, mathematicians, historians, economists, artists and regardless of whether they are Einsteins, Churchills, Beethovens, or Picassos. Whether or not Churchill develops encephalitis, he has to study math for which nature did not give him the capacity to absorb and retain or use. So that instead of Beethoven filling up the special niche in music that nature had intended him to occupy, all the information in science forced on him by unscientific science teachers would have rounded him into a ball that keeps rolling off, to sink into frustration, mediocrity in a field he wasn't designed to excel in, and finally, into oblivion. Picasso, originally gifted by nature with a sharp eye for beauty and the sensitive hand to record this beauty on canvas loses his vision and the ability to function after graduation. He is blinded and lamed, taught to look only at what the authorities see, and to do as he is told. Einstein ends up as a tramp because he can not fit anywhere after his formal schooling. His superior antennae for reading the abstract is legally nipped off by the school heads, so he would be like the rest of the antennae-less cookies in the mold their oven will cook. Luckily for mankind, the Beethoven, Einstein and Picasso of history had very little formal schooling, and so escaped this fate. Churchill, too, managed, but only after untold pain. He suffered intolerably from his schooling, but his strong genes helped him survive. Those who refuse to go to school are branded as "truants" and "delinquents" and are hunted down to be locked up in correctional institutions where they'll rot before they are dead. Those who comply and submit to this expensive dehumanizing procedure are given valueless diplomas, degrees and awards that don't even guarantee the right job for them or insulate them against bankruptcy or give them any idea of what life is like outside school.

Now this malady is caused by a virulent virus which decides to have the brain as its address. When it moves there, the owner of the brain feels an acute need to show off. Not to show but to show off; not to prove but to mislead. Suttees had to show off their love and loyalty to their dead husbands whether or not this love and loyalty existed or whether the dead man was worthy of a tenth of it. Chinese women had to show off that they were dainty and that they belonged to the nobility and were above the peasants whose labor gave them the trimmings they were so vain about. They had to show off this daintiness even if they were as coarse as, or coarser than, those they despised. Scholars (those who go to school to be certified) have to show that they have brains for higher learning, even if they don't, and so they undergo the violent process that goes on in a formal classroom—competition, standardization, submission to incompetent teachers, confusion of myths for facts, blind romance with trivia that evaporates as easily as erotic love, and negligence of basic literacy skills and the development of their higher mental processes.

This same need of having to show off is the culprit behind other crimes, old and new. People grab money not because they're physically hungry, but because they're psychologically hungry—for public approval. They can't wait for the natural arrival of the day when their efforts and positive talents will pay off, as they eventually would. They can't wait to show off the money they don't deserve because they are stricken with this mass insanity of pursuing an image. They are sick. So they grab. In the old days, grabbing was in the form of piracy on the high seas. Now it's professional swindling, hijack, politics, academic mafias.

Chasing shadows. Only dogs like the one in Aesop's fable should be guilty of this crime and should deserve to lose the meat after barking and pursuing its reflection. Not us, civilized human beings. And, definitely, not the academic dons!

The suttee has long since been stopped. Feet-binding, too. But the virulence of formal education has spread to us developing countries. And then, the Third World countries will catch it. They, too, will suffer from mass insanity. Procrustes will reign supreme in this beautiful world to deform and mutilate our children and grandchildren before our willing eyes. Will this horrible disease also take hundreds of years before it finally goes pffft?

Help!

5

The Well-Meaning Elfin
A Short Story on Individual Differences

(Published in The Magic Pencil, *1988 issue)*

ONE ENCHANTED EVENING, when the moon waxed unusually bright, a strange game was going on in Dr. and Mrs. Magdaleno Laban's yard. Whispers and faint giggles were audible aside from the usual soughing of the evening wind. This was strange, indeed, for the big antique house was empty. Dr. and Mrs. Laban had left for Manila for the former's heart by-pass operation, and Mrs. Laban had locked up the house as their only maid, Rosing, had gone with them. Iking, the town idiot, had been paid well in advance to water the plants regularly during their protracted absence.

The strange game had been initiated by Kuliling, the elfin girl who lived in the elfin mound in the Labans' yard. The week before, as was her wont ever since she could remember, she had sneaked behind the blackboard in one of the classrooms in the public school nearby, and had listened, fascinated, to the science teacher lecture to her pupils about plants—that plants need four basic elements in order to live, namely: sunshine, with which they cook their food; water, which supplies them the minerals from the ground for their nourishment; air, which gives them carbon dioxide in exchange for the oxygen they throw out; and soil, the most basic element which gives them security and the foundation from which they grow.

"Now," she said to her fellow elfins gathered about her in awe (because she was the only elfin who had gone to school), "I want to apply the scientific theories I learned from my science class on Mrs. Laban's plants while nobody is home!"

"What do you intend to do?" timorously asked Paytot, her cousin whom nobody thought much of because he didn't even know what a school is for.

"Just watch me!" she said expansively, and commenced ordering the

14

awe-struck elfins about.

"These roses are monopolizing the sunshine. Move them over yonder to the orchard. Farther—there—into the darkest corner. A change of scene will do them good!"

Huffing and puffing, the obedient elfins did as they were told.

"Now, these plants under the orchard have to be sunned. Dear me, they must be anemic by now. How they have long been consigned to the gloom! Out with them, for their own good!"

And so the pots of palmeras and Lucrecia were dragged out without too many questions.

"Now, let me see . . ." muttered Kuliling, peering in the moonlight at her notes. "What else did that science expert teach her class? Water! That's it! Plants need water as well as sunshine!" Looking about her, she spotted Dr. Laban's cactus collection in the greenhouse, perched on dry sand and gravel, as if purposely avoiding the very tonic noised about in the classroom.

"Take these poor, prickly species out to the *batalan* where they'll receive a good dose of water they certainly have long been deprived of. This will not do—no wonder they are so ugly and defensive. They had been merely rationed with such an important commodity . . . and these sweet beauties by the batalan—how could they endure the stink! Poor creatures . . . let's take them and hang them on the santol tree for a good airing. The fresh air will be a treat and they'll be so grateful for the change . . .!"

"But the santol branches are already occupied, ma'am," protested one of the impromptu gardeners. "Where will these poor orchids go?"

"Inside the compost pit!" Kuliling answered as if the problem was too simple to be discussed. "After all, too much height can cause hypertension and a plunge into the depths should counterbalance the situation. Yes, the pit is ideal."

And so the water lilies were unceremoniously uprooted, repotted painstakingly in the husk pots of the orchids and hung on the santol tree to enjoy the fresh air. The orchids were tenderly left deep inside the empty compost pit. The cacti were carefully replanted along the swamp vacated by the former beautiful tenants.

"Now, learn to float, you pin cushions! That little talent might make you as pretty as the water lilies and then everyone will overlook those ugly thorns!" Kuliling chided the cacti.

After everything had been done according to Kuliling's specifications, the elfins wiped their perspiration from their brows and congratulated her on her scholarly interests. Blushing self-consciously, she waved away their approval and said with glee, "It's time we opened Mrs. Laban's eyes to a more scientific way of gardening—according to the books used in schools. When she comes back, she'll gladly forgive our little 'trespass' when she sees the dramatic results!"

The results were indeed dramatic. When Dr. and Mrs. Magdaleno Laban and Rosing arrived home, the shrieks of Mrs. Laban upon setting foot in the yard almost undid what the heart specialists in Manila had done for her husband. The spectacle that greeted them was dismal enough, but to the superstitious trio newly released from the hospital, the implication was more dreadful: death. Their prized roses were all dead. Whereas their petals had been red, yellow, pink, peach and white, and their leaves and stems all shades of green, they were now all brown. The elegant Lucrecia whose dark green leaves were thick and velvety had become faded kropeks that, alas, could not even be eaten. The other mainstays in the orchard—the palmeras—which had been dragged out into the sun, had shriveled after untold agony. Her imported orchids had long asphyxiated in the compost pit. Dr. Laban's rare cacti had rotted in the swamp, their remains like carcasses of porcupines after a plague. Her pretty water lilies that had nodded their heads at Rosing's activities on the batalan above them now hung lifeless from the boughs of the santol tree.

It was obvious that the plants did not die due to Iking's negligence. The soil in the pots where the plants used to grow was still damp. And Iking could not himself have conceived transposing anything. He was an idiot, not a smart aleck.

"What kind of monster has played this tasteless joke?" wailed Mrs. Laban into her kleenex. "Who trespassed on my property and forced my sunbathing roses into the shade where the dark frightened them to death? Who shoved my sensitive-skinned Lucrecia and palmeras into the sun to die of sunstroke? Who mercilessly buried my orchids alive? Who hung my water lilies like common criminals?"

Turning for sympathy to her husband who must surely be just as stricken as she, she found, to her horror, a beatific expression on his pale face as he lay prostrate on the garden couch after their distressing tour around the yard.

"Rosing! Is he . . . ?"

"No, ma'am, he is still with us. Only his mind seems to be gone . . ."

Mrs. Laban was stupefied. Could his rare cacti have meant so much to him that he had lost his mind over their loss?

Dr. Laban, a retired Regional Director of the MECS, wore an expression which could have been worn by a sage during a moment of revelation. Gazing upon his wife who, like him, had spent all her professional years teaching school, he smiled and said, "My dear, you mustn't feel distressed. Nature has killed our plants so that our youth, the dear hope of our country, may live . . ." Looking at her and through her, he continued: "My brush with death has somehow illumined my mind. Now I can see very clearly what neither my colleagues nor I saw before: that for 45 years, we had played smart. We forced sunshine, water, air and soil on the pupils without bothering to find out if they'd thrive or die from a dose of all these. You were much more considerate to your plants than to your pupils, because you knew which plants loved the sun and which hated it. And with that knowledge, you took care that your sunlovers—your roses—got their fill of the sun. That your Lucrecias and palmeras who hated it stayed in the shade where its rays couldn't hurt them. That your water lilies stayed in the cool swamp where they could float and be always in the water they love. That your orchids stayed up in the air, away from the soil which threatened to anchor them and rob them of their mobility. You respected their different natural inclinations, and they bloomed, to nourish your soul, in gratitude.

"But—did you do the same to your pupils? Did I—to the youth, whose growth and development had been entrusted in my hands by our society?

"My dear, you did not, because I, the boss, the authority, ordered you to do differently. Unlike the gardener in us who sees Nature as the trustworthy book to follow, who sees plants as sacred, with individual differences and needs, the educator in us could not do the same. Overloaded with theories from our universities, we could not see nature's design for each of her children, and thus tampered with it. We ignored nature and revered our books and credentials instead. I, for one, got drunk with my power, and used you, my obedient followers, to "dehumanize" the youth, contrary to our sworn duty to nurture them and prepare them to grow up as nature had designed them to become, so that they would, in turn, nourish our hearts when we are old. We had been butchers, my dear, both of the young and the old. . . ."

Mrs. Laban stared at her husband in disbelief. "Grief causes insanity," she thought to herself. "If he is mad because he could not accept the loss of his cacti collection, then I must be mad, too, for losing more—my orchids, my roses, my—"

Her thoughts were interrupted by her husband's droning voice.

"We imposed a curriculum which presupposes that children are all alike and have no right to protest our dictums. We thought that we, because we had gone to the university, know better than they. How many pupils did we ridicule, publicly and privately (in records), because they hated math? How many did we flunk because they did not show enough interest in science or civics or culture as we demanded? How many suffered needlessly—from ulcers, migraines and encephalitis—because we forced algebra and physics into their minds which would rather have absorbed other things? How many eventually formed the habit of cheating just so we would not punish them for not coping? Did you ever punish your Lucrecias for hating the sun? Or fret because the cactus refused to take your water? Did you look down on the water lilies and the orchids for escaping from the soil? Did you ever overwhelm any of your plants with all three elements—water, air and sunshine—before they had taken root in the soil? Yet, that's what we did and still do to our pupils! We overwhelm them with science, civics and culture, even before they are rooted firmly in literacy. Pupils who are not even Independent Readers yet are already given homework in science, reading, social studies, and forced, on pain of failure, to answer questions they cannot read. Yes, plants do need sunshine, water, air, and soil. In theory. In reality, none can thrive on all these put together. Lucrecias wilt from a dose of sunshine; the cactus rots if watered too much; water lilies and orchids are better off without soil. Pupils, too, like plants, need to know science, math, civics and culture, only in theory. In reality, only a few—the future academicians—can make any use of all these subjects. As long as he is literate, the businessman can survive on elementary math alone. Will he lose customers just because he got low grades in science or history? Just because he has never heard of Edison or of Plato? Conversely, literary men and philosophers have a natural aversion to math and can succeed in their career ignoring that subject completely. Artists, for their part, need cultural exposure and so they like civics and culture. Allowed to master their particular art without being distracted by other academic subjects, they can find fulfillment better than all academicians put together. The scientist needs none of these. He expresses his genius by using his reason alone.

"The trespasser you want to lynch right now probably meant well, too. He wanted our plants to be well-rounded. Not to be good only in absorbing sunshine, but to enjoy the cool shade as well. Not to stay forever floating on water, but on air, too.

"You were proud of your roses which excelled only in one thing —sun-worship, and you didn't force them to excel in water-indulgence or in loftier activities offered by the air. I, too, adored my cactus plants which could thrive without water. Then, why could we not have been contented with a pupil who loves only literature and the pursuit of truth—a potential philosopher and man of letters? Why must we force him to prepare himself to become a businessman and a science scholar, too? And if we could leave orchids alone just hanging freely in the air and thank them for brightening up our day by doing just that, why can't we also allow Maria to just concentrate on her music and then entertain us with a fine performance in the future? Why do we have to make her know scientific formulae and dogmas that might irritate her fine sensitivity and thus needlessly harm her artistry? And why do we force a pupil who wants to be a businessman to waste his energy and time on sonnets and essays, whose irrelevance to his plans will just deplete his vigor? Worse, will annihilate other necessary virtues like common sense, to transact his business with?

"As if these were not enough, we had to follow the Americans' path to child abuse by copying their brutal stroke against the normal individual—the NCEE. The NCEE prevents a student like Carlos P. Romulo, who was poor in math, from entering college. It keeps an Einstein who was good only in physics and math from college, too. It prohibits a Pangasinense or Campampangan from entering college, if their Pilipino (which is not their native dialect) is not good. It wants to admit well-rounded high school graduates only, who are equally good in English, Pilipino, math and science. In other words, naturalized freaks. Freaks who will graduate from college as "misfits" in life. Because they're neither Lucrecia nor rose nor orchid nor water lily nor cactus, but a part and parcel of all these, who were "schooled" to grow everywhere but can thrive nowhere. Under the sun, his Lucrecia part wilts; in the swamp, his cactus part rots; in the shade, his rose part sickens; in the air, his water lily part collapses; in the soil, his orchid part suffocates.

"Now I don't wonder anymore why we have business administration graduates who don't go into business; economists who can do anything except economize; history majors who "excel" in the past but not in the present and future; science scholars who top science exams but cannot invent. Now I know why journalism graduates belabor politics and sensation instead of finer topics: they had been kept from the good books by all those required textbooks. Now I know why lawyers end up as politicians: somewhere, somehow, during their overdrawn schooling, underneath all those homework, they must have lost their sense of right and wrong, and thence, their personal worth. A 'conspicuous chair' like a senator's is indeed the best apology for such a loss. This insight is Ralph Waldo Emerson's. Now I know, too, why the number of hospital admission escalates, instead of decreases, in spite of the influx of so many new doctors and nurses: so many people are unhappy because they are in the wrong jobs. And they are in the wrong jobs because in coping with school requirements, they forgot what their original talents had been, and the fact that they ever had any. Do you remember asking me one day, with umbrage, why the more perceptive critics refer to education as the 'academic Mafia'? Now I can tell you why. It is because we educators had been fed on a diet of nostrums which we are now in turn dispersing with all formality and exorbitant charges under the pseudonym 'academic degrees'!

"My dear, what have I done? What have we done?" And, to both women's utmost alarm, the old sick warrior burst into tears.

Mrs. Laban was by now convinced that her husband wasn't delirious from grief over his dead cacti. She had listened to every word and was touched by the truth. She knelt beside him and said, "There, there, dear, what is done is done. You meant well. Yet it's not too late to do something if you feel you must. Why not tell the other MECS officials about your revelation?" To her confusion, her husband laughed out loud.

"Didn't you know that it's suicidal to tell authorities the truth? Especially a simple truth which the illiterate gardener sees, but which we, who have earned the distinction to use blinders, as all gownsmen unwittingly do, don't?" And he laughed again. He laughed long and hard at himself and at all his fellow bureaucrats.

"But," he said, checking his hilarity, "since I know that I haven't got many years left in this world . . ." And with that, he renewed his sobbing. He was weeping now for the persecution forthcoming to him and his, because he had decided to tell the truth.

Seeing him thus alternate between empty mirth and despair, and thoroughly apprehensive over the effects of the day's events on his heart, the two women broke into a hideous duet, which brought the neighbors pounding on their gate.

To their urgent importunings on who had died, for heaven's sake, Rosing honestly answered to the best of her knowledge: "Our beautiful plants."

Dr. and Mrs. Laban were still in a tumult and could not answer more truthfully: "The youth."

Postscript

What happened to Kuliling? Well, she shut herself up in her mound after her experience with scientific theories. To her unending vexation, her fellow elfins, especially those who had never stepped inside a classroom, but read a lot in private, refer to her as a "science scholar" instead of "scientist" as was her original ambition. She had no way of knowing, of course, that however disastrous her applied theories were, they nevertheless provided the catalyst in evolutionizing the country's school system.

Genetics and the Required Curriculum

DEP'T OF AGRICULTURAL EDUCATION
AND RURAL STUDIES
University of the Philippines at Los Baños
College, Laguna, Philippines
28 May 1988

Dear Mrs. Hamada:

Dean Villareal and I were still talking about our interaction with you even on our way home last Friday. It was indeed very nice meeting and talking with you and actually seeing your place as well as some materials you are using in your innovative educational progress.

We read with some amusement your story and those of your wards and I must admire your single-mindedness and dedication in publishing *The Magic Pencil*. I think it is a unique way of encouraging the children to improve their communication.

Your modest facilities, which correspond with your modest fees, confirm my notion that it is not necessary to have a luxurious environment in order to bring about effective and efficient learning. The printed study materials and a well- knowing teacher are indeed the basic ingredients.

Yet I find it important to reiterate to you my belief, which is grounded in psychology, that learning is dependent on the approach and not on the learner's genetic make-up. While it may take a longer time for a slow learner to learn calculus, he can learn it and any other complex stuff for that matter, if and only if the correct approach is used by the instructor.

I have validated this psychological truism in my own experience teaching delinquent boys in Michigan as a teacher aide some years back. I was able to turn negative attitudes to learning into positive ones by applying correct psychology and the boys under my charge learned arithmetic.

I am looking forward to your next book. We need more critics of our educational system so that we can force some change in the right direction.

Do come and visit our beautiful campus. Hope to see you again in the future. Good luck on your trip to the U.S.

Sincerely yours,

HIGINO A. ABLES
Professor

P.S.
The pictures will come later.

Gino

Harvent School
Lingayen,Pangasinan
27 June 1988

Professor Higino Ables
Dep't of Agricultural Education and Rural Studies
University of the Philippines at Los Baños
College, Laguna, Philippines

Dear Prof. Ables:

I'm in the midst of a flurry characteristic of an imminent overseas trip, but I found time to write back and thank you for your letter of 27 May 1988. Thank you for reading my short story in *The Magic Pencil*—it's the first and only story I've ever written and I hope it didn't sound too hysterical in my effort to underscore my plaint about "required curriculum."

You reiterated that a learner's genetic design may be overridden by the right approach and an understanding teacher—but is it really

23

imperative to make pupils learn everything and exhaust all ways and means for them to learn something they'd rather not learn at the moment? This is the main crux of this letter: the necessity, not the method of instruction. Neither am I talking about negative attitudes per se; it could be that the pupils with negative attitudes you handled had the genetic capacity for math and calculus. I am talking about pupils who are willing to comply with math requirements but who are genetically not equipped to learn it or delve into the subject matter. It is for these pupils that I articulate the question and why I challenge authorities on education about prescribing a "required curriculum" without first looking at existing facts like individual differences. You are talking about delinquent pupils. I am talking about normally behaved pupils who have natural preferences that may not fall within that set of required curriculum. Don't they have the right to pursue areas of special interest and to protest when pressed to pursue areas they're indifferent to? Again, I may not get the answer to this. Neither can I presume to give one. But I am already happy that I have provoked one such as you to think and write me his thoughts.

I have finished my article on the National Language issue. If you want a copy, I can send you one. Just use my address here and they'll forward your letter to me in the U.S.

I visited your beautiful campus in 1984, but I'd love to see it again if I get the chance. Meanwhile, you think you can give me a NEEM tree seedling? I've read so much about it and I wish I could have a seedling or two and get a taste of the many benefits from its many virtues.

Regards to Dean Villareal—I wrote him a long letter—and I hope to hear from you both again.

Sincerely yours,

Margarita V. Hamada

24

Can Science Be Taught?

28 MAY 1988

Dr. Ruben L. Villareal
Dean, College of Agriculture
University of the Philippines at Los Baños
College, Laguna

Dear Dr. Villareal:

Thank you for your visit with Prof. Higino Ables last 26 May. Because we only had limited time to discuss my views on education that you read in my book, *School Mythtakes,* I wasn't able to elucidate some of the points you considered worth challenging.

First, about the Philippine Science High School—you told me you are still impressed with it because most of its graduates are usually topnotchers in universities they eventually graduate into. That's just it. I deplore this very fact that said science school produces topnotchers and scholars, not scientists and inventors. Scholars are not the scientists we need, and it's a pity because they could have become the producers we need if they had been allowed some freedom to do things on their own and not processed by that science school. As you would find out from my new articles I furnished you and Prof. Ables, a science scholar and a scientist are two very different people. A science scholar masters a certain structure (the school's) and a pattern of thinking and doing things (the school authorities') and falls into the habit of obeying, instead of challenging authorities, because his attention is fixed on evaluation, not on the task at hand. Hence he gets excellent grades, but loses, in the process, his unique outlook that leads to invention.

Now, a scientist is usually an outcast of the school system for refusing to comply and be processed. He scoffs at the patterns of thinking of his teachers, textbooks and fellow students and the "standard" procedure they impose on him to follow. George Bernard Shaw approvingly described the great scientist Galileo in these words: "Galileo denied the infallibility of Newton and destroyed human faith in absolute measurement, and played tricks with the velocity of light." This is because a scientist is so original and different in his attitude and approach to a problem. "His intellectual advances," continues Shaw, "may present themselves as quackery, sedition, obscenity or blasphemy, and always present themselves as heresies." Hence, he could not excel in science schools, much less fit there. So, he either bids adieu to his originality, curiosity and independence and becomes a scholar or gets kicked out. On his own, he can freely produce amazing new products, ideas and technologies. He feels limited by the two-way structure of learning (teacher-class) and feels insulted by the whole set- up, knowing that science is an intellectually active process that involves the search for new information and not the acceptance of old information. In simpler terms, science is nothing but curiosity. Who can teach this mental process? Who can teach curiosity as a subject? Can science be taught? I bet education authorities have never asked themselves this question. And if they will, because I have asked it first, they'd say yes. Which is funny, because the answer is NO. As Roger Cunningham's *Science: Focus on Process* (Curriculum Development in Nongraded School, Goldnew Venture, 1971) articulates, "To present science to children in an intellectually honest manner, it must be presented in its true form. To present it as factual information misrepresents it. The facts of science are constantly and rapidly changing, but its processes are stable." Therefore, to teach pupils scientific information without first determining if they're interested, compelling them to memorize such information and to prove that they have, through quizzes and tests, and by recording their scores and computing their quality point average is the WRONGEST way to produce a true scientist. (Note: The author is happy to annotate here that exactly a year after she wrote this letter, her statement that "science can not be taught" was validated by the results of the Regional Achievement Tests conducted by the DECS Region I. Addressing heads of schools last 24 May 1989, in San Fernando, La Union, the Regional Director, Dr. Gloria Z. Lasam announced with alarm that pupils fared very poorly in science. (See?) Not sharing my conviction that science can not be taught, she promulgated an urgent change in the curriculum, making the teaching of science 60 minutes every day, instead of the usual 40 minutes. The author predicts, for reasons she has already explained, even poorer results from this new regulation.)

I thus find the whole idea behind science schools deplorable and wasteful. Scholars are so easy to produce—all schools actually give their yearly share without fail. They provide our problem-riddled society with a bumper crop of honor students and academic awardees each year, who ironically add to, instead of lessen, its problems, unfailingly beating agriculture in providing us with a bumper crop of the more necessary commodity—rice.

But scientists—people who think, challenge and act—are so rare that we should use funds like the kind directed to science schools to nurture this breed, not to kill them off, because it is to them that we owe most of our creature comforts. This is what I mean by questioning the existence of the Philippine Science High School and its value to our country. If it's only good at producing scholars, and can hardly produce the kind of men we call scientists and inventors whom we urgently need, I feel misled and defrauded as a taxpayer, by its very name. It shouldn't be called Philippine Science High School, but something like Philippine High School for Academic Excellence or Philippine Military School for the Mind, and must not be funded heavily for this shallow purpose. So much for this topic on science.

Now about pressure in learning. There are two kinds of pressure: external and internal. To absorb any skill or information, we need pressure, but certainly not the external kind—like compliance for fear of failure or for the sake of credentials. We need only one kind of pressure—and it is the internal kind: initiative or desire to learn.

Growth of any living thing is always from within, not without, so it is vital for the child to want to learn, when he wants to. No educator, no matter how multi-awarded he or she is, can effect learning to take place in a child who is there because of external pressure—parental or social. Hence, compulsory education is really a big joke.

External pressure is necessary only for inanimate objects. A nail cannot join two pieces of lumber together unless hammered from the outside. Are pupils inanimate objects who need to be hammered by grades and compulsion so they can learn? The experts insist they are, because they can not tell the difference between apparent learning and real learning, for all their studies about education.

Pupils who refuse to learn may not yet be ready. Period. Because of individual differences, a pupil may be ready to learn only after puberty or even long after that. What right do we have to change nature's design? What right does anyone have to take this against him? Parents and school heads must face facts, not myths—that mental growth/receptivity to learning does not occur to everyone at the same time. If we do this, learning would be less "bloody" and we'd be sparing ourselves unnecessary stress.

Taiwan's progress may be due to its citizens' desire to progress—and this is pressure from within—the only force or power that results in growth. They may have been externally pressured, as you have observed, in your 18 years' stay in that country, but this external pressure must have been an offshoot of their initiative and desire for further improvement, not the cause. What do you think?

Learning is such a fulfilling activity that we do not need to use external pressure if we only leave the learner to discover its joy. But we don't—before he even gets the chance to discover it, he already resents it because whether he's ready or not, we compel him to go to school and to study, or else . . .!

One last word—real learners, who are not necessarily scholars, inevitably become producers and entrepreneurs—their own boss. Scholars usually find themselves employed, with these real learners as their boss.

My whole philosophy intends to produce more learners, not scholars, because citing myself as an example, self-employment is more rewarding than employment, financially and psychologically, and gives one the leisure to achieve more, whereas employees have to wait for their retirement—when they're 65, for a taste of this leisure which I have enjoyed since I was 29.

My philosophy doesn't aim to make producers/entrepreneurs of everyone. It aims to sift prospective producers/entrepreneurs from the ordinary employee and get them out of the delaying, flattening process that might reduce them to mere scholars and employees.

May my fellow-learners like you share my vision and help me remove the obstacles towards its fulfillment.

Thank you again for your very stimulating visit to Harvent School, and looking forward to more of it in the future.

Sincerely yours,

Margarita V. Hamada

Discipline and Freedom in Learning
or
Why We Handle Science and Social Studies Differently

WHO OF YOU feel cheated by your "studies" in school? I do.

I studied science for at least ten years—six years of Elementary Science, two years of General Science, and a year each of Biology and Physics. I topped my class in these subjects as a result of the efforts I put in due to my irrational fear of being beaten by my rival—which was a feat for a girl who'd rather have played and read comic books. My efforts were wasted, however, because I did not acquire the scientific attitude or value that I could have used in meeting my personal needs.

The same is true with social studies. This subject was listed in my report cards for eight years as follows: Philippine History, Philippine Government, Oriental History, American History, Rizal, Philippine Social Life and Progress, Economics, etc. Yet, after graduating as valedictorian, I was just as naive about human nature and the ways of the world as if I had never left my mother's womb. As a result, I had to break my heart many times over real social situations because these said subjects I had studied so painstakingly had failed to develop in me the perspective that could have made me cope effortlessly with said situations.

To put it bluntly, I became unscientific because I excelled in my science classes. I also became temporarily disoriented with society for exactly the same reason: in my pursuit of excellence in social studies, I removed myself from the company of people and defrauded myself of the necessary exercise in social relations.

The things I got instead, from my studying very hard, were things my parents and I did not bargain for because they are of no use to me or to anyone else—an amnesia of what I had studied, a phobia for studying, and a loss of faith in school authorities. Why? These authorities had made me waste my time and hopes. They had taught me those subjects without considering a very important fact about learning, and therefore

I failed to achieve the purpose of those courses. And the fact they missed is this: Learning progresses on two feet: discipline and freedom. A student succeeds in learning an academic subject and profits from it only if he completes the learning cycle consisting of three stages:

1. Romance (first stage of freedom)
2. Precision (period of discipline)
3. Generalization (final period of freedom)

Since a cycle consists of two stages of freedom and only one of discipline, the reason for my misgivings is obvious. My school had taught me science and social studies without giving me the necessary background of freedom. Alfred North Whitehead, from whose book, *Aims of Education,* I got the important facts about learning, warns us that:

Without the adventure of romance (freedom), at the best you get inert knowledge without initiative, and at the worst you get contempt of ideas—without knowledge. (Exactly what I got!) But if the stage of romance has been properly managed, the discipline of the second stage is much less apparent, that the children know how to go about their work, want to make a good job of it, and can be safely trusted with the details.

Let us then define the three stages of learning, so that we may make our children's education consist of a continual repetition of such cycles and thereby assure their success in learning their subjects: romance, precision, generalization. Freedom, Discipline, Freedom. Whitehead defines romance or the first stage of freedom for us:

The stage of romance is the stage of first apprehension, with possibilities half-disclosed by glimpses and half-concealed by the wealth of material. In this stage, knowledge is not dominated by a systematic procedure. Its essence is browsing.

In Language, the child goes through this stage of romance by listening to stories, songs and poems and by participating in conversations with people around him. Whitehead now defines the stage of Precision, or the period of discipline for us:

During the stage of precision, romance is the background. The stage is dominated by the inescapable fact that there are right ways and wrong ways and definite truths to be known. This is the time for pushing on, for knowing the subject exactly and for retaining in the memory its salient features. It represents an addition to knowledge. This stage is barren without a previous stage of romance; unless there are facts which have already been vaguely apprehended in their broad generality, the analysis is an analysis of nothing. In this state we acquire other facts in a systematic order, which thereby form both a disclosure and an analysis of the general subject-matter of the romance.

In Language, this precision stage, according to Whitehead, gradually increases concentration toward precise knowledge of language—grammar, spelling, vocabulary. At the end of this stage, the children should have command of English and should be able to read fluently. "Thus," continues Whitehead, "precision will always illustrate subject matter already apprehended and crying out for drastic treatment."

Finally, Whitehead defines the last stage of learning—the stage of generalization or the final period of freedom:

> At this stage, something definite is now known, aptitude has been acquired, and general rules and laws are clearly apprehended both in their formulation and their detailed exemplification. The pupil now wants to use his new weapons—it is effects he wants to produce. In this sense, education should begin in research and end in research. This stage is a return to romanticism with added advantage of classified ideas and relevant technique.

In Language, at this stage of generalization, Whitehead says that the language study is confined to "reading the literature with emphasized attention to its ideas and to the general history in which it is embedded."

We must also take note of another important fact disclosed by Whitehead: "That no pupil completes these stages simultaneously in all subjects." He illustrates this fact for us:

> For example, while Language is initiating its stage of precision in the way of acquisition of vocabulary and of grammar (and spelling), science should be in its full romantic stage. The romantic stage of language begins in infancy, with the acquisition of speech, so that it passes early towards a stage of precision; while science is a latecomer. Accordingly, a precise inculcation of science at an early age wipes out initiative and interest, and destroys any chance of the topic having any richness of content in the child's apprehension. Thus, the

romantic stage of science should persist for years after the precise study of language has commenced.

At this point then, parents should look at "studious" pupils with alarm, and not with admiration. For it is during these years in the grades and in high school that he must only familiarize himself with the wonderful world of science and social studies, and must not be distracted by efforts at precision in these subjects. Scientific procedures, scientific laws and technical data are not supposed to be in his scope of learning during these years. They must be reserved for his "study" at the right time—in his future college work.

The duty of educators is therefore to acknowledge that different subjects and modes of study should be undertaken by pupils at fitting times when they have reached the proper stage of mental development.

They must teach Language in its precision stage in the grades and in high school, and must require pupils to master grammar, spelling and vocabulary while yet in said elementary and high school. At the same time, they must introduce science and social studies to them in the romance stage of these subjects—telling them stories about animals and plants, people and places, watching films about these, going on field trips often, exploring all interesting things they see and hear, browsing through terminologies, and just traipsing through the wonderful world of science and social studies. No quizzes, no homework, no demands for scholarly activity in these subjects in the grades and in high school. Educators must be ready with future developments that "towards the age of fifteen (just before college), the age of precision in language and of romance in Science draws to its close, to be succeeded by a period of generalization in language and of precision in science."

Had my school been aware of Alfred North Whitehead's insights and discoveries, so much waste could have been avoided during my schooling. But they could not be aware because the DECS officers are also ignorant of this most important fact on learning, despite their academic degrees and years of being the authorities in education. Had they been more concerned about real learning, and not its counterfeit—certification—they would have been more receptive to new ideas like Whitehead's, would have been more consciously seeking newer insights, and would have applied their discoveries for our benefit. I could have become a writer at age 13 rather than at age 31, and would have had in my possession a good grasp of my world without having had to play truant in my household work to get it. I must share the lessons from my memories of my schooling and Whitehead's observation to caution parents and educators that "the result of such an undue extension of a most necessary period of development was the production of a plentiful array of dunces, and of a few scholars whose natural interest had survived the car of Juggernaut."

I was lucky to have survived, but not without permanent emotional scars. Some of my classmates have been crippled for life! And my pupils in Harvent School will be lucky, too, for if the errors of the schools I attended prevented me from profitting from my lessons in science and social studies before, my memories of my wasted efforts and the enlightenment I got from Whitehead as to why, shall deliver the lessons properly to them.

9

The Meaning of My Elementary Education
and What I'll Do with It

(Address delivered by Regina L. Sison, aged 11,
Harvent Schools' Achievers' Day, 20 March 1988,
Sison Auditorium, Lingayen, Pangasinan)

DISTINGUISHED GUESTS, PARENTS, TEACHERS AND SCHOOL-
MATES:

Thank you for coming to celebrate with us our achievements. This
afternoon, 23 of us shall receive our Certificates of Competence from the
Founder/Director of Harvent Schools.

What does this certificate mean? It means much more than having
attended grade school for six years, because some of my classmates and
I who are about to receive it had spent just three to four years instead of
the usual six years. Harvent Schools' different technology enabled us to
save that much in time and money and effort.

It also means much more than having finished the standard elementary curriculum, for our curriculum in Harvent School is richer than the
curriculum prescribed by the Department of Education. The curriculum
I finished in Harvent had been purposely designed to produce thinkers
and skilfull communicators. And so, my certificate means I can think
well and write and speak well. In other words, my certificate confirms
the purpose and meaning of elementary education—which is, the
mastery of basic communication skills and the possession of a positive
attitude to polish these skills and use them purposefully. That is why we
learned English as three separate subjects—1) Developmental Reading
which developed our vocabulary and comprehension skills, 2) Grammar, and 3) Spelling.

That is why we had extra subjects like Journal Writing, Story
Telling, and Sustained Silent Reading in the library which took up my
whole morning every day, Mondays to Thursdays. And we had Journal

Correction every Friday. Every morning, for an hour, we read books of our choice in the library. Then, for another hour, we challenged ourselves by writing about a certain topic—a scientific phenomenon we had discussed in our Science class, a curiosity that had cropped up in our Civics and Culture class, or an unforgettable story we had heard or a movie we had seen. And, at every schoolyear's end, we saw what we had written in our journals in print—in our very own magazine, *The Magic Pencil*. This inspired us to love the habit of writing. And lastly, we had Science and Civics and Culture in the form of stories—as mere reinforcer of our English subjects and not as basic subjects, so that we would not get diverted from the chief purpose of elementary education.

My certificate also means I had participated in activities that developed my personality and my ability for self-expression. In 1985, I annotated a number in the program for our Achievers' Day. In 1986 and 1987, I danced and sang. This year, I helped choreograph our dance number for you. For the past three years of my stay in Harvent School, I wrote and illustrated my entries to our magazine. I worked on my workbooks and revised my mistakes every afternoon. I shared secrets with my friends and exchanged jokes with my teachers in between. I offered solutions to real problems. I asked questions. I worked hard on my drills and lessons in school and never at home, and I played most of the time. Thus, I blossomed intellectually, socially, physically and morally.

Now it's time to use what I gained from grade school more responsibly, as befits a truly educated person. What shall I do with the skills in communication I have acquired? I must not allow them to lie fallow and waste the coming years memorizing information which I'll just forget. I must not allow them to rust while I plough through rifts of "required" subjects irrelevant to what I want to become. No, I must polish my skills by using them for more substantial things than passing tests and completing requirements for a high school diploma and/or a college degree. I must use them to open more roads for me which can lead to prosperity and fulfillment. I must commune with great minds by reading, reading, reading on my own. My elementary education has honed my skills in vocabulary and comprehension. And it has also sharpened my ability to think for myself and to differentiate between what is excellent and what is not. I have come to know that for me to learn about science, I must consult no less than the best scientists and physicists—and they may not be found in the classroom. Science teachers in the classroom, no matter how zealous, are not the scientists or physicists I want. They are merely holders of a BSE degree, major in Biology or Physics. To me, they are not the best. They might even hurt my curiosity and enthusiasm to learn. They might embarrass me for looking at matters differently. I want teachers no less than Albert Einstein himself, or John Van Neuman. But they are dead, you say. I say, they are not. They still live, for they have immortalized their thoughts in the books and articles they have written. And these books are free for anyone who has the key and the willingness to use this key to open them, and the capacity to appreciate their vision. I have the key. I have this skill. It came from my elementary education from Harvent School. And I will use it.

I want to know man's history—his struggles with the past—how he has struggled to make nature his slave, and not the other way around. The problems he had to face and triumph over. And to know about his triumphs and defeats, I must seek the help of the best historians. Again, my friends, they may not be found in the classroom. For the ones I shall meet there, no matter how earnest in their job of teaching history, are, again, mere holders of university degrees—BSE or AB, MA, PhD in History. The historians I seek are Arnold Toynbee, Will and Ariel Durant, Gibbon, long dead and gone—yet alive. Their thoughts pulsate in their books, which I am welcome to examine and explore at my leisure.

I also want to learn about the meaning of life, in general, to meet philosophers who can explain and share with me their views on life and existence. And again, I may not meet them in the classroom, for the philosophers I seek belong to a rare breed and may also have long passed on. They are the great ones whom universities cannot afford to hire—but whom I can afford to meet—in the library, between the covers of their books: Ayn Rand. Bertrand Russell. George Bernard Shaw. Ralph Waldo Emerson. Buddha. Jesus Christ. Aesop. They, too, like the great scientists and teachers, have immortalized their thoughts on paper—and I shall happily polish and enrich my elementary education by constant reading, and use it to get a full glimpse of the scope and depth of their minds. Then I can enjoy life more fully and shall smile more.

Yes, I shall use my communication skills responsibly and fruitfully. I shall use these skills to earn much money so I can give, and need never ask. Not by enrolling in renowned business schools—for I am told that no graduate from the Asian Institute of Management or the Wharton Business School has yet become a millionaire, but only hired hands for millionaires. But by observing actual millionaires at work, talking to them, reading about their coups, and applying their success formulae in my own endeavors.

I shall use my skills to pursue higher and richer knowledge—in science, history, philosophy and business outside school. To interact with great people in society, for I have developed the personality and the confidence necessary to enjoy their company and wisdom. Not to allow my future schooling to drown my mind with conventional impractical details. Not to allow my ability to think, ask and challenge to be submerged by rules and regulations formulated for people who refuse to think or who cannot think. To keep on reading inspiring stories so I shall know how to distinguish between right and wrong, good or bad, so I shall not be unnecessarily delayed from becoming an asset to all of you.

I now say good-bye to the happy, stress-free years in Harvent School, which gave me the skills, the maturity and independence I now have, for my bright tomorrows to spring from. When I shall have used these gifts as I have outlined, I would have said my thanks to my Alma Mater most eloquently. My huge debt shall have been paid.

Again, thank you for coming and I hope you'll enjoy the program we have prepared for you.

Good afternoon to all of you.

10

Who Needs a College Education?

EMPLOYEES' AVERAGE annual income, together with their spouses', suffices for their basic needs—food, shelter and clothing. They should be glad. But they aren't. They are close to despair because one commodity they value so highly cannot be covered by that income —college education for their children. These employees want desperately to send their children to college because they also believe, like most Filipinos do, in the persisting myth that a college degree is a ticket to a better life. But, deep inside, their reason is—everybody's children go to college. Even the tricycle drivers' children go, so my children have to go, too, so they won't feel left out. People look down on anyone who did not finish anything.

My annual income will, of course, allow me to send my children to college. These employees must envy me because I can afford the commodity they can hardly afford. But they're in for a big shock—because I wish I did not have to send them to college. I love them too much to submit them to an institution that will just confuse them about the direction they want to take in life; that will deaden their common sense and imagination; that will just delay them from becoming what they want to be in life.

College, at best, prepares students for jobs. And I don't want my children to spend their precious time and energy and my precious money only to hold a job all their life afterwards. I want a career for each of them, and education outside school can give it to them more effectively and more quickly at the least cost: actual apprenticeship in several jobs (yes, I don't mind them holding jobs before college—because then their purpose is to learn, not to earn yet), visits to museums and galleries and other places of interest at their leisure and initiative, travel, and all the hours to read what they want at home, or at the public library, at their leisure.

The education I have chosen for them could be free or more expensive—travel abroad is almost prohibitive, but, at least, I get my money's worth. Putting travel aside, the other sources of education outside school are free. And the big bonus I'm after is this: my children would have four years' headstart in life over their peers. Those who had chosen to go the long way by enrolling for a college degree would only start thinking of how to live after college. My children would already have that knowledge; the work field is unbeatable in this line of discipline. They would also have already defined what exactly they are good at, and would have mapped out the outline towards becoming who they want to be by that time.

Whereas their peers who went to college would find out, the way I did, after spending a little fortune and four or more years of their lifetime, that what they did was something not crucial to their future—complying with course requirements that standardized their thinking into patterns and which rounded them off instead of making them grow according to their naturally intended shapes; and socializing, which they could have done better in the work force or anywhere else. They'll also find out, sadly, that they had missed reading many good books because their schoolwork occupied most of their time; that they were not able to see a beautiful movie relevant to the times or to their personal growth because they had to bone up for those exams; that they could not meet and interact with people like Christian Barnard or Robert Frost or Mahatma Gandhi because they were in the classroom, listening to the pratings of lesser persons called professors; that the lessons forced on them by the Department of Education could not help them get along better with their mothers-in-law or give them the income some self-made people who did not even finish high school enjoy. They'll wonder why they gave away so much in time and money, energy and hope, to get almost nothing in return but a diploma whose usefulness is, they learn too late, doubtful. "Personnel managers of the world love to see BA, MA, or even PhD on your job application," says Helen Gurley Brown, a self-made woman who skipped college but made it to the top via the publishing world, "but those degrees don't necessarily get you even the beginner's job you want," she points out. "Your college degree won't even make you a whiz in your first job," she cautions. "What can you really do for a company until you've had a chance to work there?" she asks, common sensically. They'll also find out that certain values and myths they have a hard time shaking off their systems have come from school—from their professors who are geniuses at robbing their students of the ability to think and refute what they preach, but who are absolute dunces in making them future assets to society—and from their fellow students who have mortgaged their brains for a diploma, and therefore are incapable of producing new theories in lieu of wornout myths.

College graduates, because of so much studying during four years in school, assume a false sense of competence and superiority, confirmed and validated by their diplomas. This could work to their disadvantage. They'd feel too qualified for a beginner's job which would have given my children the solid foundation from which to grow into the company, and the map which will direct them to where they want to go as they progress in specialized knowledge and know-how. Hence these degree holders drift from job to job, dissatisfied, frustrated and defeated (victims of heart attacks, the main cause of which is job dissatisfaction), unlike my children whom I would have spared this mentality and hence this sad odyssey.

I have read about and even personally known many persons who started off as janitors or messenger boys in a company and ended up as owners of the same, afterwards. Ergo, I have also read of and personally known persons who, after getting an MBA or a PhD, got stuck in a very limiting managerial position or deanship. Some were even "demoted" due to the Peter principle which says that people fail or become incompetent when they keep getting promoted until they reach a level that is too much for them. MBA or PhD degrees automatically open "too good" positions for their holders who may fall short of their demands, because their degrees do not necessarily reflect their true abilities.

Because of all these reasons, I can hardly bring myself to sacrifice my children in support of collective opinion and habit that sees college education as a necessity. I wish they are exceptional enough to make me decide they should skip it. Because if they are not, I'd be forced to send them to college. For how else could unexceptional people get a job without this expensive credential? Only exceptional people need no credentials because they themselves are their own credentials. But if they are exceptionally spunky like Helen Gurley Brown, Aristotle Onassis and Henry Sy of Shoemart, they'd surely earn the delicious privilege of succeeding in life without college credentials. Then I won't send them to college. Like George Bernard Shaw, I'd also rather be criticized and persecuted for thinking and doing differently than be like them and be liked by them but "suffer from their stupidity and illnesses" in return. After all, I'm not going to watch them bum around (Pardon my street language which I picked up in college). I'll see to it that they work, travel, and meet people. That way, they would unfailingly be able to "detect when a man is talking rot" or not. "For that," in the opinion of Harold MacMillan, former British Prime Minister, who quotes his professor at

Oxford (not all professors are dumb, by the way), "is the main, if not the sole, purpose of education."

"Many learn without being taught."
—John Holt, *Freedom and Beyond*

41

11

Self Education Beats Formal Education

(Address delivered on Harvent Schools' Achievers' Day,
20 March 1988, Sison Auditorium, Lingayen, Pangasinan)

MY DEAR INDEPENDENT READERS, elementary graduates and their proud parents:

Good afternoon. Congratulations on our achievements this year. I say "our" because your children's achievements are yours and mine, too. Thank you for having entrusted their early education to Harvent School, thereby giving us reasons for joy today. Not all parents think the way you do—you wanted education for your children, and not just the certification most people want; and our schools' non-graded policy and competition-free technology gave you what you have sacrificed for. Our being different from other schools did not frighten you from supporting my ideals and now we have this moment of triumph and fulfillment to celebrate together.

But I have observed that whereas you wanted real education for your children in their early years, you now want formal education for them hereafter. Some of you have asked for your children's clearance so they can take the entrance exams in schools in Dagupan City and Metro Manila where education is more formal and, you suppose, better. Where, you suppose, they will be better prepared to pass college entrance exams and tackle college work. Because of this, it seems to me that you have suddenly become less ambitious for your children. Your goal of giving them a formal education is no longer as substantial as your goal when you enrolled them a few years ago in Harvent. Then, you wanted real education for them—literacy, and the development of their higher mental processes of independent thinking: observing critically, analyzing, synthesizing, choosing, imagining, questioning and communicating their thoughts coherently. We delivered all these to them. They can read and write and compute because we drilled them mercilessly in the skill subjects we call Basic Reading, Developmental Reading, Language, Spelling and Basic Math. They freely observed, criticized, analyzed, imagined and asked because we do not impose standardized answers in their information subjects like Science and Civics and Culture. We did not ask them to memorize any information in these two areas and never asked them to disgorge such information in quizzes or exams. They were never afraid to give their insights on things they'd read or heard of because we respected their opinions and never frightened them with evaluation.

Now, you want to give them a more formal education complete with grades and awards and diplomas. Have you ever stopped to think if formal education is a good legacy to bequeath to your children? Have you ever asked yourselves what formal education could really do to them, or consider a very startling fact—that it could actually harm them? Have you ever paused to reflect if there is anything far superior to formal education that will truly be worth pursuing because it will unfailingly lead your children to more fulfilling careers, and not just jobs, and thence, to richer, fuller lives?

I am saddened to see that you haven't. And because you haven't, I feel you are remiss in your duty as parents.

Dear parents, my precious pupils. There are two kinds of education available for you to choose from: formal education, which could be had by attending schools, colleges and universities at great cost, and self-education, which could be had anywhere for free. Which of these two is more effective and worth pursuing?

Let me answer my own question by recounting to you my own personal experience with formal education and what it did to me:

When I was just two years old, my father, the erudite Juan Ventenilla, Sr., predicted that I would become a writer. I saw things adults normally do not notice, and remarked on these with a maturity that amazed and amused my elders. Then I went to school. There, I compromised my extraordinary gift for something less extraordinary —academic honors. I graduated at the top of my class from grade school to high school, but lost, in the process, most of the sharpness, originality and maturity I had displayed as a child. In the novel *The Ambassadors* by Henry James, Chad, a character in the story, is described as a victim of formal schooling and its required disciplines that authorities erroneously consider a must to be studied if one hopes to develop his mind. But, alas, like me, "study had been fatal to him so far as anything could be fatal, and his productive powers faltered in proportion as his knowledge grew." Like Chad, my productive powers were almost extinguished. During those 14 years I spent in formal schools, I did nothing but memorize information and do as authorities required. My thinking powers and natural gift for original insights atrophied as my scores in exams shot up with vigor.

It wasn't until many years later when, freed from the useless demands of my formal schooling, I decided to make up for those wasted years by leisurely reading. I didn't know then that reading on my own was self-education, and that it would beat my formal education a hundred times. But it did. My self-education enabled me to really learn what my schools had failed to teach me, and allowed me to successfully shake off the damaging effects of formal education on my mind and personality so that I was finally able to fulfill the promise that had been glimpsed in me as a child. My first book, *School Mythtakes*, was published in 1987. My becoming an author was late by twenty years, so I could hardly forgive my schools for having required me to study math and science subjects at the time when my natural turn for Letters should have been encouraged and allowed to run its course. I honestly believe that because of their impositions on me to become a well-rounded person—good in everything—which isn't at all what nature had intended me to be—I became a rolling stone that gathered no moss for ten solid years—1969 to 1979. Yes, ladies and gentlemen, I lost ten years—years when I could have made a name for myself in the media or the literary world, but didn't, because of my formal education.

Like you, my parents did not stop to probe deeper into the merits and demerits of formal education. Had they done so, they would have seen and anticipated and thereby would have prevented the harmful lifetime effects of what they were so eager to let me go through. I would thus not have undergone four useless years of college and become a rolling stone afterwards as a result. I would have had all the time and leisure to read those great books years ago and would have profited from them and would have become the truly educated person I now am, earlier.

For, ladies and gentlemen, contrary to what you think that I owe my present status and stature as educator and author to the schools I attended, I do not. I owe my present stature to my self-education because I made up for the limitations of my formal education by reading for learning and enjoyment, not for compliance, and so I learned. Helen Gurley Brown, editor of *Cosmopolitan* magazine, and one of the 25 most influential women in the U.S., also discovered that "listening to experts and working out in school are simply delaying tactics." Therefore, unlike me, she skipped college and worked straightaway and became what she is now—successful and truly fulfilled.

But poor me—I went to college. There, as in high school, I had to study science—and I did not learn anything because my teachers were not scientists but science teachers. I had to study history and instead of learning about the fascinating panorama of man's struggles with his environment, I learned to memorize useless, unrelated historical dates and events and thus resented history as a subject. Instead of improving my wisdom and perspective, history in school depleted my mental energy with trivia that I could not relate together. This is because my teachers were not historians but history teachers. I only discovered the true joy of learning history and profitted from its lessons by myself, when I read, out of curiosity, Michener's *Hawaii, The Source,* and *Texas;* Haley's *Roots;* Mitchell's *Gone with the Wind;* RD books like *The Last Two Million Years, Great People of the Bible and How They Lived, The Churchill Digest;* Durant's *Lessons of History,* and many others. These books were written by historians, achievements which our history teachers can not do, so I learned history much more effectively than I did in the classroom.

Therefore, like Helen Gurley Brown, neither do I recommend workshops, seminars, night or even college courses. Because, like her and others who attended those, they did not get us anywhere near our big dreams.

Now, with this conviction—that self-education is more effective and worth pursuing than formal education—I cannot rest unless I share it with you, and inspire you to really think hard first before you make your children suffer the same unfortunate delay and stress many others and I underwent. I warn you of the dangers of formal education which took its roots from the collective need that sprouted from industrialism. We are now in a more demanding era called super-industrialism which demands thinkers and truly educated people, not rolling stones and mental/moral cripples that formal schools produce in plenty. Some of you here want your children to be "advanced" in science, so you will enroll them in science schools, without looking hard at your child first if he or she is naturally cut out for the sciences or not. I truly challenge you if your child will ever advance in science that way. He or she will merely become unscientific. Instead of becoming a scientist, he or she will end up as a science scholar. We do not need science scholars, dear parents. We need scientists—young men and women who will question, challenge and act. Not young men and women who will answer test questions, prepare to be questioned with great anxiety, and cannot act or invent on their own. We need scientists, so I beg you to ask this question first before sending your children to science schools: Will they be encouraged to think and experiment in their own way and to refute their teachers or will they be expelled if they don't "do as they are told"?

Now, it's your turn to ask me: What will our children do if formal school is to be avoided? My answer is: Many productive things. They can polish their skills in reading which we at Harvent School have taught them, by reading anything at random. They can also freely explore the study of science at their leisure. To study science, the whole world is the classroom. Nature is the best teacher. Leisure is the best method. TV, museums, good books and magazines, and curiosity and logic are the best instruments—not science laboratories, textbooks and a dogmatic science teacher.

Science, history, economics and higher math are unteachable. They are self-learned by anyone who is interested in learning about them. For this self-learning, which is a far more enjoyable and effective activity than attending formal school, Harvent School has equipped your children with the best instruments—communication skills and the maturity and self-confidence to use them well.

You must have noticed by now that your children, who are only elementary graduates, can communicate better than some certified "professionals." They think independently, write well and speak well. For this, my staff and I deserve your thanks. For we taught your children the basics and polished these, instead of emphasizing the less important information subjects. We are not proud of students who are "advanced" in science because we always wonder: Can they make anything out of all the knowledge that may be true today and false tomorrow? And we sincerely doubt if they would know how to write down their thoughts coherently or read new theories with understanding, if their time had been put to "studying" science rather than "learning"—reading and thinking and expressing their thoughts.

On this special day, I exhort you, my dear pupils whom I have watched blossom intellectually and morally under my philosophy and methods, and you—their parents—to see to it that the skills we have taught are not wasted. That the maturity and independence and self-confidence developed in the stress-free atmosphere of Harvent School are not killed off by grades and competition and requirements of formal schooling.

Use your skills. Read on your own, and you need not go to high school or to college. You can beat any scholar produced by any science school by just reading leisurely and experimenting on your own. You can become richer than any graduate of a business school by apprenticeship where you can observe actual business operations. Some became millionaires by putting up their own businesses when they were only teenagers. You can reach success earlier if you read what is most interesting to you and stay out of the classroom longer. Self-education is better than ten university degrees. Great Britain's first woman Prime Minister says the same thing: "Self-education counts for much more than the education you receive at school."

I shall feel proud and not feel that my efforts have been in vain if at least one of my graduates will become a self-educated person, a person who loves to read and doesn't stop learning, and therefore learns what these formal schools can never teach him. I shall have been thanked most eloquently, and with him in this world, I shall not be afraid of the future.

Congratulations again and thank you for coming. Remember, the things your children will ever need have already been given by us at Harvent School. They are now ready for the only true education available – self-education. Don't delay him or misdirect him by insisting stubbornly on a supposition that has long been debunked. Read and grow with your children and improve your luck and mine and the whole world's. But a word of warning—self-education has no end. You'll never graduate nor get a certificate. You won't care to, anyway, when you and your children will have discovered the joy of true learning. Good afternoon to all of you.

12

Nationalism or Chauvinism?

(Published in the Manila Bulletin, 16 January 1989)

DO WE REALLY have a national language? Is Filipino a language or a dialect which our nationalists are dressing up to become the national language we sadly do not have?

Culture grows parallel with its language. Filipino culture, unlike Japanese, Chinese and European cultures, never developed to become like said cultures because it had been destroyed by repeated foreign incursions into our shores. Hence, we have no single unifying language, but a diversity of dialects—which reflect the reality that our culture had been smashed into splinters. Inevitably, our present culture is now the culture of our former American conquerors, and we find ourselves living a lifestyle reflecting that culture. This is why we speak English, which is not just a language, but an international language, to keep abreast with the Western culture we had been woven into.

A linguist said that one can think better in his own native tongue. True. But one can also think best if he had more words at his disposal. And the English language provides a well-stocked arsenal for anyone in this planet who wants to tackle not only the literary, but the technical, philosophical and metaphysical areas of life. Does Filipino cover all these in its scope? No. Because it is not yet as established as the English language, and is still growing (by borrowing English and European words), it will be hundreds of years before it can reach the status of the Japanese or Chinese, English or European languages. So, why do we require Filipino to be the medium of instruction in our schools? Is it because there is merit in this allegation—that "Filipino students learn best if courses are conducted in Filipino"? This statement remains an allegation until it is proven. Absorption of knowledge does not depend on one's ability to learn. It is one's interest in a subject matter that really determines one's success in learning. If I'm not interested in Economics or in automobile mechanics, I can never learn it even if it was translated into my own dialect. Two young men I know, who are not experts in the English language, learned computer science and word-processing from manuals written in English. They learned because they were interested in learning, not because the subject matter had been translated into their native dialect, which it wasn't.

So why insist on the undeveloped just because it's ours? Is chauvinism nationalism? Should you use the bolo when a chain saw or the laser is at hand? We use the bolo for cutting bamboo. The chain saw or the laser would be superfluous in this case. We use our dialects for ordinary conversations and simple business transactions within our region, and to express our soul in songs and literature. Any other language would sound put-on in this situation. But when we have to learn or impart technical, philosophical and metaphysical knowledge, we have to switch to a more effective tool—a language. Like the chain saw, a language can cut through the hard timber of ideas more efficiently. Like the laser, which can plow through sensitive tissues that gross instruments fear to tread, a language like the English language can open our minds to higher levels of consciousness and pit us against subtle issues like Time, Space, Existence, Transcendence, Quantum theories of energy. We use steel bridges, septic tanks, airconditioning (which are products of Western civilization), and our life has become richer and more comfortable because these are now part of our life. How much more progressive can we get if we mastered the English language we already have, rather than funnel our energy and resources to transform a dialect into the language it is not?

The Philippines, as a nation, has far to go in terms of economic progress. Some blame it on our lack of a national language, and not on Marcos or on the kind of discipline or collective consciousness we have. I'd like to share this observation: Those who speak only their native tongue belong to the poorer sectors of society—in their own, and in the world's: Mexico, Puerto Rico, Africa; whereas those who have achieved individual progress inside or outside their nation's boundaries and are contributing much to the world's progress as a whole are the ones who speak English very well. The Japanese send their children to international schools if they can afford to do so, because they realize that Japanese who speak English aside from their own language are better off anywhere even in their own country, than their countrymen who know only one language—their own. Ergo for Europeans, South Americans, Arabians, Chinese, Indians and Filipinos. They, like many progressive-minded Filipinos, have accepted the fact that we are not only Filipinos, Chinese, Japanese, etc., but international citizens, and as such, must know how to communicate with one another accordingly.

Rizal's reprobation that "a person who does not love his native tongue stinks like fish" is not applicable if we realize that we do love our own dialects (in my case, the Pangasinan dialect), but not necessarily Filipino, which is not native to me and to all of us.

We have not thrown away our bolos and our bamboo structures, so I'm not advocating that we throw away Filipino just because it is a dialect. I am just questioning the compulsory presence of Filipino in the curriculum and in the NCEE. Everybody learns his own native tongue and an extra dialect or two without the help of the school. Nobody wants to pay good money for something one already has and/or one can get for free. Its imposition as the medium of instruction will hamper the younger generation from effectively learning a very difficult but helpful tool—English. Unless we make English the medium of instruction in our schools, from preschool to college, it is impossible to master it. Remember, we tried to learn Spanish by having had it included as a subject in our curriculum before? Well, I got top marks in all my Spanish subjects, but I cannot speak it fluently nor use those lessons I got from the classroom to understand and appreciate Julio Iglesias' beautiful Spanish songs. Hence, the education authorities' plan to teach English in this same ineffective way as Spanish had been taught will result in the same useless consequence. Filipinos will lose a valuable tool or asset—that of having English as their other language, which, may I repeat, is not just a language, but an international language, and a MUST if they are to become the productive residents of a bigger village called the world. For we have expanded our village or nation from its boundaries to include the whole world. We live where we please. Many of our relatives now live abroad, most of them in English-speaking countries—U.S.A., Canada, Australia, South Africa, England, Malaysia, India, Hong Kong, Indonesia.

If my elders' exclusive love for the bolo will prevent me from benefitting from the mastery of the use of the laser, and thereby making me a misfit in this global village I now live in, then their kind of nationalism is not just pseudo-nationalism, but chauvinism. Its virtue is not only questionable, but obsolete, for we are out of industrialism for which nationalism was a necessity. We are now in globalism. Furthermore, nationalism is not localism. It is love for one's country, its welfare and its growth. Since modern times have made our country and other countries,too, for that matter, transcend their old, original territory, we must also love the corresponding language which helps us function anywhere and ties us all together in peace, harmony and progress.

In my recent three-month stay abroad (U.S.A. and Japan), I observed that Filipinos abroad hold better jobs and bigger responsibilities than other non-English-speaking nationals from Mexico, Puerto Rico, Vietnam, Thailand, etc. A young man from China who sat next to me in the plane bewailed this sad fact in his broken English: "It fearsome difficult for Chinaman to go abroad because his English is very small."

We cannot, therefore, afford to be arbitrary in matters concerning nationalism and how we should show it. If we force students to learn Filipino when they'd rather learn English because they value and appreciate its significance in their lives, they will just resent Filipino. Would our nationalists like that?

13

Illiteracy in the U.S.A.

*(Address delivered Achievers' Day, 2 April 1989,
Sison Auditorium, Lingayen, Pangasinan)*

DISTINGUISHED GUESTS, dear parents, members of my staff, my dear pupils:

During my visit to the United States last July, I became aware that we in Harvent School have a unique blessing in spite of our economic problems: we have a very effective technology for literacy which U.S. schools don't seem to have.

The U.S.A. is a very rich progressive country, the leader of nations in the world. It has the most advanced technology in industry, electronics, science and medicine. But despite all these advantages, I was shocked when confronted with its problem that is not at all in keeping with its strides—ILLITERACY. Advertisements on tv, billboards, print ads behind the covers of bestsellers and inside magazines keep reminding everyone that one out of three adult Americans cannot read or write. I don't know how accurate the statistics are, or whether the media is merely dramatizing the problem in the hope of getting the teacher-volunteers they need. What I can say is, illiteracy should only be expected in primitive regions, not in a country which represents the height of civilization—but it is there, sticking out like a sore thumb in the grandeur of the United States. Finding this problem in the USA is like finding a venereal disease inside the walls of a nunnery!

The Americans of course are concerned, or else announcements would not have been made at such great cost. They fully realize that if they do not lick this problem fast, their status as a world power will decline. Their growing illiterate population cannot make use of their computers and sophisticated science laboratories. But most important of all, the very foundation on which democracy rests—literacy—is disappearing. With it will also disappear the following: awareness of important issues, further achievements, intelligent participation in government and world affairs, and ability to think and steer one's life and the world, towards the right direction. In a capsule, illiteracy spells DISASTER for this great nation.

With this first-hand knowledge of the debilitating effects of illiteracy on any society, rich or poor, I want to congratulate the parents of my Independent Readers, my grade school graduates and all my pupils and each of my staff, for their concerted support of Harvent School—whose chief aim is to deliver literacy to each of its pupils despite severe financial constraints and the demoralizing influence of the existing system of education which values certification more than the literacy we value so highly. Please accept my congratulations, high esteem and profound gratitude. And please share my optimism for further achievements in the years ahead.

Years from now, when the world, not just the Philippines, moves on toward its promised "Golden Age," we would know that our support for literacy would have had something to do with it. The children whose minds and personalities we have nurtured would be among those well-equipped to propel society to its destined Golden Age. Please accept my congratulations again and my gratitude for your cooperation and for the simple fact that you understand Harvent School's priorities.

It is true that we still don't have a gym and some modern apparata for science. But we make up for these with our superior instruction force and facilities in literacy. In the US, the opposite is true. Their schools have beautiful gyms with shower rooms, swimming pools and saunas, computers and the best audio-visual facilities. But these are all an incongruity because, according to the media, their instruction in literacy is weak.

It is true that the modest fees you can afford cannot give your children these facilities yet, but we can do and actually have done something about this minor problem. Already, we held a raffle draw last Christmas. I'd like to thank the parents who donated the prizes for that draw. We also held a popularity contest which generated the initial amount for all our dream facilities. My heartfelt thanks to all parents of the candidates for Mr. and Miss Harvent School '89, namely, Mr. and Mrs. Ramon Arcinue, Mr. and Mrs. Rogelio Paiso, Mr. and Mrs. Orlando Caneja, and Mr. and Mrs. Ruperto Antonio for working hard in this fund- raising. May the joyful memories of today's coronation rites in your children's hearts be always the sweet reward of your efforts. If all our parents can show the same spirit as you have, we can have all our facilities completed soon. As of today, our facilities for literacy are complete. I choose the best teachers—those who are proficient in written and oral English. We have reading kits which only Harvent School possesses. We have SRA kits, a library of imported books and magazines, workbooks in Developmental Reading, Spelling and Language, daily storytelling of inspirational classics, daily drills in self-expression through journal writing and formal themes.

Delivering literacy is not an easy job. It cannot be done through computers and tape recorders or films. It can only be done through our method—personalized, competition-free, with due respect to individual differences. This is indeed a difficult method, but we have no choice because the elementary and high school years are mainly for this purpose, not for the rote study of the sciences. Literacy, not scientific knowledge, makes an educated person. And only in the hands of an educated person can discoveries in science be put to good use. Only an educated person can learn science and other disciplines and use it for the benefit of mankind.

I would appreciate it if the parents would come to my office and tell me their ideas and suggestions so that Harvent School can best deliver its ideals. Your rapport with me is just as important and decisive as the fees you pay. Harvent School's existence saves you a lot of trouble. You don't have to hire tutors for your children. You don't have to do any homework for them because they do everything in school with our supervision and guidance. Supporting Harvent School, then, through effective dialogue with me is supporting your own personal comfort.

Let us help one another make life easy during these hard times. In this way, we shall all be in good shape to enjoy the better times about to come.

Thank you and good afternoon to all.

14

Values or Instincts?

VALUES OR INSTINCTS? Which of these two should be developed in the pupils by our Department of Education? I ask this question because the DECS' verbal emphasis on values education has become farcical in the light of what they are actually espousing. Through oversight, perhaps, more than a fault in values (this is what I prefer to think), the DECS has, on several occasions, given official sanction for instincts to triumph over values. What instincts are these? Mercenary instincts. The dictionary defines "mercenary" as "having love of money as motive; working merely for money or other reward." Whereas "values" are "qualities on which worth, desirability, utility, depend." Gratitude. Loyalty. Good will. Honesty. Hard work. Friendship. These are values. Travesty on these should alarm the DECS and must never be allowed, much less officially. For we have painfully arrived at civilization where barbaric instincts like piracy, treachery and unscrupulous conduct have no place, especially in the world of education. But take a good look at these cases:

Several teachers who earned their keep for years at Ateneo de Manila University left the said institution and founded their own school. The DECS gave them permit to operate, because, apparently, it overlooked some sad points: their school opened in the same area their former employer is servicing. This means that they intend to siphon off a considerable number of the prospective enrollees of the institution on which their subsistence depended for a long time. Put more simply, the DECS helped them cook the goose which had given them their eggs. It sanctioned their ingratitude, their disloyalty, their mercenary instinct to make money at the expense of none other than the hand that had fed them for years. By giving them a permit to operate as a business rival of the source of their well-being, the DECS allowed them a convenient shortcut (the morality of which is questionable) to money-making. What hard work is necessary now that they attract enrollees by capitalizing on the good name and trade secrets of the institution they came from? The name of that institution they are using to sell their school had been earned through years of honest hard work and fidelity to values. And now, through the DECS' approval, all they have to do is ride on its prestige. Values? Hard work? Of what use are these to them if there is a better, easier way of making it? Their advertisement in the papers reads: "We are a group of seasoned educators from Ateneo de Manila." The flaw here boiled down to this: Why did they not open their school somewhere else—say, Cebu, where they would not have to steal the market from their former employer? Well, it would be inconvenient for them. You see, they are not familiar with the Cebuano taste and mentality as they already are with the community which Ateneo is servicing. And, of course, there may be just a handful of Cebuanos who can afford the fees Ateneo charges, unlike in Manila, where there are more. That means, they would have to start from scratch, and that would be hard work, considering that they have a shortcut as an option. However, this shortcut means getting what they want at the expense of another—and this "another" happens to be no one else but their own benefactor. Is this flaw very hard to see? Is this flaw allowed to flourish in the world of education?

In Paranaque, Sylvia Chan (not her real name), owner of Children's Learning Center (not the real name), hired her best friend as Assistant. She trained this friend and taught her all her bag of legitimate tricks. Not long afterwards, this friend of hers put up her own school and pirated most of her friend's pupils, conveniently using (what else?) the former's good name and trade secrets. She was allowed to do this, officially, by the DECS.

In Region I, this case had been repeated. Former employees of Advance School (not the real name) had been given permits to rival their employer. Two of these, who had been with said school for 20 years, applied for their permit "stealthily," while yet connected with Advance School. Treachery has been unwittingly sanctioned officially. Like the former teachers from Ateneo de Manila, these three former teachers of Advance School find it more convenient to dump gratitude, friendship and loyalty in favor of the opportunity of using the prestige Advance Schoolhas built up through the years. After all, if they put up their school in Ilocos Norte, where they would not have to steal the market from their former employer, they would have to do it the way the owner of Advance School had done it—the hard way.Who would know Advance School in that far-flung region? They'd rather take the shortcut and run over their former boss, using her school's name and methods to attract pupils who would otherwise have enrolled in Advance School if they were not siphoned off by them.

A DECS officer in Region I put up her own school, contrary to the DECS rules and regulations which guard against "conflict of interests." She could not wait until her retirement, which is still a long way off. So she went into partnership with her elder sister, whose retirement from DECS allowed her to be co-owner of said school. She pirated the Assistant of the owner of another prestigious school, who, in turn, engineered the piracy of five of her fellow-employees and the pupils of that school by using the full trust and confidence given to her by the owner who was her best friend. Together, these people have conspired against their former employer who had done them no harm, whether personal or professional, by writing anonymous letters to the DECS, denouncing the school for certain irregularities it had never committed. One letter, which was nothing but libelous, was signed by four of them; the owner-victim has sued the four in court. The DECS officer whose sister is posing as the owner of her school campaigns for pupils and poormouths the other school from whom she pirated her staff. Her best friend, who is also an officer of the DECS, has access to the official achievement tests that the division office uses to gauge the different schools' performance in delivering literacy. Leakage is therefore very likely. Her school might top the tests, but illegally—through leakage. Her school was given a permit to operate pre-school and grade school in spite of the fact that her building does not conform to the specifications of the DECS, all because she has friends in the office that issues permits.

Now I ask the DECS: What values can the pupils of these unscrupulous business women absorb from them? Is it right to give permits indiscriminately? Is it right to officially allow hardworking educators to be run over by human sharks like these? Is it right to expose innocent pupils to their wicked morals and watch them become just as mercenary as their models? Where would these children eventually lead our society to if this is tolerated by the authorities? How do these cases fall in with the DECS' frantic call for revival and development of human values?

The DECS is right in fostering healthy competition to ensure quality education. It is right in encouraging more entrepreneurs to solve the problem of unemployment. But must it achieve these goals in cases where it is done at the expense of educators who have already proven their worth in the field? Should it give jobs to a few teachers at the expense of hundreds of pupils whose spiritual growth will be threatened by the example they see? Remember, values are caught, not taught. Must it give sharks an easier chance to succeed where people with good morals and right values are made to struggle and bleed?

If the DECS can answer these questions (after all, education is supposed to lead to the ultimate skill of distinguishing between right and wrong), but cannot act on them, our society that created this expensive machinery will be sorely shortchanged if not totally ruined. Let's watch and see.

15

Maturity: The Foundation of All Values

History, the sciences do not yield up
their secrets to the immature.
—Ralph Waldo Emerson

Characteristics of:

A Mature Person	An Immature Person
gives	gets
admires	envies
achieves	competes
trades value for value	demands more for less or something for nothing
leads	bullies
is realistic and practical	pretends
grows from his errors	deteriorates progressively
does not impose on others	seeks attention
does not want to impress	commits crime to impress
is honest and forthright	backbites
thinks	believes
is peace-loving	is unharmonious
is emotionally stable	easily gets hurt
is financially independent	is a moocher
is self-sufficient	depends on others for his/her happiness
knows solitude	knows loneliness

does not blame others
    for setbacks
	always blames others
	    for setbacks

enjoys life	suffers

won't allow anyone to rob him
    of choice
	robs himself voluntarily
	    of choice

creates	destroys what he can't equal
is not afraid of the new	is full of fear
solves his problems	runs away from problems
succeeds in spite of obstacles	fails because of similar obstacles
is an asset to society	is a liability and headache
is positive	is negative
asks	condemns
discusses	argues
is open	is close-minded
challenges	accepts and hopes
acts independently	obeys or disobeys

Maturity cannot be taught; it can only be caught—from mature people. But immaturity, which is the seat of evil, can be easily fostered. It is being nurtured in schools which applaud competition, obedience, acceptance of facts and rusty beliefs. Maturity can be killed. And this is being done most effectively by our schools by not allowing free discussions and free choice, by inculcating fear in the pupils through evaluation, by expelling thinkers from the campus and by emphasis on externals like records, and valuing appearances like diplomas in lieu of real learning and ability.

How could schools teach values when they destroy their very foundation—maturity? How could an immature person be honest, creative and confident? How could he give when his immaturity enables him only to get? How could he be realistic when he is trained to look only at externals and appearances? How could he think and survive when he has been habituated to accept, obey and believe? How could he ever be happy when he cannot achieve, because he knows only how to compete for others' approval—and to destroy that which he cannot do? Remember what Mary McCarthy says about destruction and immaturity in her book, *The Humanist in the Bathtub:* "The only form of action open to a child (and to an immature adult) is to break something or strike someone, its mother or another child; it cannot cause things to happen in the world . . . violence becomes a substitute for action."

If we want to have a less violent world, then we must start eradicating everything that hampers maturity. We must do away with the graded schools' system of mis-educating the young. NOW.

16

Difficulties We Have Overcome

(Editorial, 1987 issue of The Magic Pencil*)*

"BE DIFFERENT AND BE DAMNED." Harvent School dared to be different and it was damned. For seven years it struggled with persecution from different sectors, after which it discovered that it had grown not just in spite of them but because of them. In other words, it had thrived on persecution and dares for more.

What exactly were those difficulties it wrestled with through the years? Let us go back in time and remember . . .

The intelligent people who understood what we were doing and fighting for scoffed: "Why do you have to open their eyes when you can make money out of their blindness more easily? Leave their eyes closed and let them go on dreaming! Just make money out of them as the others are doing!"

The parents whined:

"But why don't you give any homework?"

"And why don't you let my boy graduate yet? He's already 12 and has been here for six years already! So what if he hasn't mastered those skills yet? His cousins from other schools have not, and they have graduated!"

"My son is always playing in your school. What will he ever learn?"

"I just don't understand what kind of school you're running. It doesn't look like any of the schools I know . . ."

"But why don't they have quizzes and exams in Science and Civics and Culture? They might flunk in high school or in college if you keep on spoiling them this way! They must know all those information contained in those areas. I want my child to be advanced in science so he can enter a science school!"

61

The MECS added to the parents' confusion by taking a long time to grant us government recognition and (believe it or not!) going out of their way to warn parents that "Harvent School is not recognized, so you'd better enrol your children elsewhere . . .!"

Here again, their false values rear their ugly faces: certification is put above real learning which Harvent is trying hard to deliver. Recognized schools do not necessarily deliver real learning, because parents complain that they have to tutor their children at home or else their children will not learn the basics; but because they comply (on paper, and in actuality) with the MECS' rules and regulations which go against the individual child's interest and development, they are given recognition. Recognition of what, I ask. Of blind obedience and subservience to government authorities who are not really for the individual child's education, but for mass education, which I have said is learning's counterfeit. Our being different and our stubborn resistance to conform must have unnerved them.

And the neighboring schools showed their fangs at our being different and at our pride in being so and reaping results they could not equal. When we opened a branch of Harvent School in Dagupan City in 1984, they banded together and opposed our good intentions of providing Dagupan City with an alternative school by writing a letter to the MECS and asking the authorities to prevent Harvent School from operating, due to its black propaganda against traditional schools. When we were allowed to operate by no less that the Minister himself (Jaime C. Laya) who, because he was a layman in Education, could see the merit of our efforts, they scared parents of our prospective pupils about the difficulty in transferring to regular schools all because we are non-graded—that they have to go all the way to Manila for placement tests to determine their grade level (See how obsessed they are with classification and certification, not education?), etc. And when some pupils of ours transferred to their schools, they made remarks to the effect that our pupils flunked their exams, and had to be accepted on a probationary basis (*kuno*). And those who excelled in their schools in spite of flunking the entrance exams were not given the honors they deserved because they lacked residence (*kuno*).

But the worst persecution came from our shaky economy itself. When our tuition fees last school year reached P2000 a year, 40% of our school population dropped out and transferred to schools which charged lower, some as low as P700 per annum.

This school year, however, much to the chagrin of our detractors, prospects for Harvent School, both in Lingayen and in Dagupan City, are as bright as ever. Our enrolment showed an increase of 42%. The MECS has finally granted us the much-delayed government recognition which parents set such store by (Blame it on our paper/credential mentality). The MECS had no choice. Our pupils scored 50% to 100% higher than the mean established by their office for private schools in 1984. Parents, bless their minds, which they have grudgingly opened, have now reversed their dialogues:

"Thank you for not having promoted Julius blindly. Now he can spell words that some high schoolers cannot."

"Chad is tops in Ateneo de Manila. He even beat the honor students there who are older than he and who are always studying, while he is always playing, as usual . . ."

"Lizza is doing even better than her older sister and brother ever did. And to think they are more studious than she."

"I think there is truth in what you said. Roscor Joy at age nine is now through with elementary school, and she did it in only four years without homework and without threats of failure. She qualified for a scholarship in high school, and is at the top of her class. I know some 17-year-olds who can hardly pass the NCEE and yet have been so obedient and studious . . ."

"Well, we have to admit—Harvent is the only school of its kind where we can relax while our kids really learn—and they're so relaxed about it, too."

The MECS superintendent, Dr. Micaela Andres, recently said when she gave a talk during our Achievers' Day last March: "Congratulations for perfecting a strategy for Mastery Learning and for implementing it successfully in your two schools. You are so far ahead of us. . . ."

The reasons for our having overcome all these difficulties are many. First, nobody can argue with success. We have consistently produced Independent Readers in English without tutoring at home in half the time and cost it normally takes other schools to do so. Parents are not that blind not to see these concrete proofs of our claims. Second, the result of the MECS Achievement Tests last 20 to 22 March 1984 showed that Harvent School's mean is unusually high. Third, our colorful parades since 1981 truthfully displayed our energy and creativity and our unique approach to a child's world. Our Achievers' Day every March showcased our pupils' public speaking ability, talents and self-mastery. Many schools have since imitated our original idea of a five-year-old emcee. Fourth, our Library which represents the best of imported children's books put finishing touches to our efforts in Language and Developmental Reading. Most important of all, *The Magic Pencil* proved to be a most effective vehicle in conveying proofs of our pupils' literacy, independent thinking, wholesome personality, and fascination for written expression.

Finally, we lowered our tuition fees this school year by 50% and won back many of our pupils. This gesture touched the heart of our community which is now ready to see Harvent School as an able ally in its fight against illiteracy and false values and as a true friend in times of financial distress.

Let the dogs bark. Our caravan marches on. . . .

17

The Non-Graded School in a Capsule

*(Lecture delivered to the Association of Educators
of Negros Occidental, University of St. LaSalle,
Bacolod City, 13 October 1989)*

GOOD AFTERNOON.

I am very pleased to be among fellow educators and parents from Negros today. This trip and this lecture are part of the intangible rewards of my having had enough anger against the schools I had attended to start my own school which is their antithesis.

My pleasure today will be doubled if I see in your faces the familiar shock of recognition upon hearing my rather perilous insights and questions about education. All of us have gone through the same experience, the same violence, the same confusion wrought by graded schools, and so I assume we must now have the same insights and questions.

My talk today will just articulate for you all that you must have asked yourselves at one time or another but never got around to discussing in the open.

Today, I am going to be your spokesman. I shall dip my fingers into your subconscious where more dangerous thoughts have been banked, and show you that these thoughts are perilous only when left deposited there forever. So I am going to draw them out for you.

Today, we are going to look at an alternative way of educating the new generation. Yes, there are alternatives. And they work. And they are much more effective and beautiful because they nourish, not destroy. They do not hurt the way we were hurt.

It is time we reject something if we find it to be wrong, and not be afraid of the difficulties this will entail. It is time we re-evaluate and re-define what education is and what we want it to do for each of us and for our own society.

This is what I am going to do for all of us here today. To help you do just that, so that afterwards, you'd be in a surer position to initiate changes and develop your own system to embrace those changes.

What I am going to talk about this afternoon is MY way or system. After my talk, I hope you will know what is YOUR way. For as Nietzche has said, "THE way doesn't exist."

Let me start my lecture this afternoon with a description of my school. The building is a modest two-storey semi-concrete L- shaped structure. It has no divisions because we have no classrooms. There are blackboards, yes, but they are hardly used. The tables and chairs we have are all movable which we rearrange according to the need of the hour.

The pupils (the beginners) do not know how to sit down for more than thirty minutes. They stay outside the school building two-thirds of the time, and PLAY, so that a visitor commented that Harvent School is a perpetual recess school. The children look happy and are happy. They are happy because they are learning, not studying. They do not have the timid, obedient demeanor of pupils enrolled in traditional schools. They have no homework. They have no report cards. They have no textbooks. They have no grade classification. They have no exams but daily drills which do not call for cramming. They do not know what an honor roll means. BUT: they learn more effectively than their less fortunate peers enrolled in traditional schools. Results of the DECS Achievement tests in 1984 showed that my pupils outperformed the traditional pupils by as much as 100 percent in the subjects tested.

The fast learners become Independent Readers at age four-and-a-half or five, and finish the six-year elementary course in just three years. Every year, we have grade school graduates who are nine years old or ten. The slow learners may take four times longer to master the basic skills, but they eventually do, without experiencing failure or anxiety or developing an inferiority complex in the process. Our pupils are active. As I said, they cannot sit still for longer than thirty minutes. But they are not rude nor are they smart alecks. They do their school work independently, with very little guidance from their teacher. No two pupils share the same schedule. They do not take achievement tests at the same time. A pupil gets promoted every day, not just in March. They revise their own errors, and therefore are not afraid to commit mistakes because we do not hold their mistakes against them. On the contrary, they learn from their mistakes. They are not uniformly well-rounded. They each have individual shapes. You see, we prefer Einstein, Beethoven, Picasso, Churchill, Romulo, to summa cum laudes and academicians. Why is this? Because we know that great men are lopsided, not well-rounded. They excel in only one or two fields, not in every field. Summa cum laudes excel in all their subjects and are well-rounded, but few are great in life outside school. This is a fact history keeps repeating and which we should therefore not ignore. Our pupils as young as six contribute entries to our publication, *The Magic Pencil*, which showcase their struggle to master communication skills in English, and their creativity, plus their original, therefore refreshing, perspective.

The teachers in my school never lecture, shout or scold. They don't prepare lesson plans. They don't record anything in their record books except the attendance of their pupils. They give equal attention and time for each pupil, so parents cannot buy them with gifts because they give no grades. They are proficient both in oral and written English although some of them do not have college degrees. They spend their time in actual teaching and sharing of ideas, and only ten percent of their time in reporting their pupils' progress to me. This gives them the time to read for growth at home. They don't make exams. They correct skillbooks as pupils answer them. In this way, feedback is immediate. Errors are pointed out, explained why they are errors, and revised by the pupils. The psychological reward these pupils get is renewed every minute as they work.

Their parents do not have to hire private tutors. They do not do any homework for their children. They relax after a hard day's work as their children develop their minds and personalities. They do not worry about their children failing or getting poor marks because there are no report cards to make them do so. They save a lot in terms of money, time and mental energy.

The system I use is the non-graded approach. I think this system is the only moral way to educate the individual child as it respects individual differences, which is the basis for a strong democracy. The system does not accelerate the fast learners but allows them to go through all the skills as fast as they can or as slow as they please. It is what Nouwen calls a "redemptive," not a violent process of learning because there is no competition, failure or rewards. The system does not just prepare the child for college work; it makes him live life at the moment, and experience the thrill of achievement every moment, thus preparing him for the greater challenge called living, not just college life. The system promotes the child to the next skill only after he has mastered the previous one. This is called Mastery Learning.

The system evolved out of my philosophy of definite definitions. First, I defined my goals. Who do we teach? The child, NOT the class. What is the reason for this choice? The class is a non-entity. It is soulless, mind-less, life-less, whereas the child is a living entity, and only a living entity can be taught. Only a living entity can think and learn. What do we teach? Skills, not information. And in the pre-school and grade school, we teach Basic Skills—literacy skills, composed of decoding and encoding words, which fall under the subject Basic Reading and Writing, and numeracy skills, or skills in numbers. That's all we teach. In the grade school, we carefully define the subjects we teach. We teach Developmental Reading skills which include vocabulary skills and comprehension skills, and Communication skills which include grammar and spelling, and, of course, elementary mathematics which emphasizes the four basic operations. The importance of these skills can't be overemphasized. Graded schools cannot teach these basic skills as effectively without help at home because they emphasize information subjects rather than skills. Why is this so? Because information is easier to handle than skills. Information can be given to a class of fifty or more, and then retrieved, unlike the skill subjects which require personalized supervision and can only be seen again when applied. This is in the wrong direction because information cannot be taught. It can only be shared, to be stored, manipulated or discarded by the individual pupil according to his purpose in life. Its importance therefore is only relative, not crucial. What subjects teach only information? Science, Social Studies (History, Civics and Culture) and Religion. Who of us in this hall is qualified to teach science? Religion? History? None of us. For us to qualify to talk about science, we must be scientists, renowned in our own field of work; for us to to talk about religion, we must be doctors of theology of a particular creed; for us to teach history, we must at least have written about a particular epoch whose reverberations can still be heard up to the present. Are we any of these? We are not, and we must not pretend to be, and inflict this make-believe role upon our pupils.

How do we teach? We teach through personalized instruction for beginners, workshops for graders (lectures are not useful at this point yet), all according to a Master Plan, not a lesson plan. Why? Because of individual differences which no lesson plan can embrace in its limited, standard scope. What do we intend to produce? Lifetime learners, not graduates. Education, not certification. Unknowingness, not knowingness. And in order to produce these products, we must define terms carefully. What is a school? Is it a formal institution where inert knowledge is dispersed on pain of failure, a jailhouse where you must spend your teens in? Or is it a center for leisure-time activities where learning takes place without one's knowing it? Regarding competition: whom do we compete with? Our fellow-learners, or with problems and obstacles to effective learning? What about discipline? Is it defined as learning or conforming? Are the terms learning and studying the same or different? Do we realize that learning is fun, that it enhances one's creativity, and that its end result is achievement? And do we realize that studying, on the other hand, is entirely different from learning? Studying is oppressive and makes one's faculties dull because its activities are streamlined into conforming to authorities and complying with course requirements. Its end products are: resentment towards learning, disorientation, and decay, not growth. What about the terms teacher and pedagogue? Do we know which of these personalities to prefer? A teacher is master of a skill and knows the legitimate shortcuts in imparting it. A pedagogue is one who attempts to teach information without the proper depth and perspective necessary for relating that information to one's life and for making use of such wealth of information. Now, let's define processes. Thinking and believing are still sadly interchanged by many of us in academe. The process that opens the mind so it can support life is thinking. This is a very difficult activity to do. Now, the process that closes the mind and induces decay and death is an easier activity or mental process. It is called believing. Here, we must re-examine the purpose of catechism and why we teach religion in our schools. We must also distinguish between a scientist and a mere science scholar. The scientist thinks and suppports life. It is a fact that we owe all our creature comforts to scientists. The science scholar, on the other hand, believes his teachers and books and switches off his mind's motor. His mind decays and dies. His academic honors become his epitaph, and frankly, he is better off dead than alive. Of what use is he to life? And, finally, we must define the goods or tools we order from schools which we can naturally use in life: education, or certification? Education is the intangible tool or equipment needed to succeed and be happy in life. It is the ability to use our brains productively. Certification is the tangible "proof" of education, which is, more often than not, misleading, for it comes even without genuine education. It can be bought by money or politics. With it, people will think you have brains, even if you don't. If your goal in life is to misrepresent, then this commodity may be useful. Some people make their way through life via appearances, and these are the buyers of that paper product.

The reason why this system is not as popular as the graded system is simple: its rewards are hidden, not obvious, because they develop mental processes which ordinary mortals' naked eyes cannot see. These mental processes that get developed by the non-graded system are the ability to choose, compare, differentiate, observe critically, explain, summarize and analyze—processes that get killed off in the competition and standardization of the graded system. In the non-graded atmosphere of learning, self- knowledge and self-acceptance emerge and get the chance to blossom. Development of maturity, which is the seat of all values, is another hidden reward of the system. A child who knows himself, his limitations and capabilities and accepts himself, is showing maturity. With this value, all other values issue forth—self-respect, self-confidence, self-reliance, self-mastery, creativity, zest for living, and the energy to achieve. All the ingredients of success and happiness.

It produces well-developed, not well-rounded individuals, whose lifelong activities alternate between learning and achieving, and challenging ideas, systems and traditions that have served their time. With the full development of the individual, we automatically get a better society, one of true democracy, for the system enables the individual to triumph over the group, the class, the masses. It enables the individual to annihilate collectivism, which is the breeding ground of communism.

My talk today, although consisting of unorthodox ideas, is not for anarchy and strife but for peace, progress and happiness. I am a thinker and I have dedicated my life to produce thinkers. I am not for destruction and death (which happens only when society is deprived of thinkers) but for redemption and life.

Thank you for providing me with an excellent audience.

18

You're Not Alone!

7 BURGOS ST.
Vista Verde Executive Village
Cainta, Rizal
15 March 1986

Dear Ms. Hamada:

Thank you very much for the nice excerpt from your book, *School Mythtakes.* The best thing I read in today's *Manila Bulletin.* We need more women like you.

May the good Lord bless you and your family always. HAPPY EASTER.

Most sincerely yours,

Perry V. Dalao

* * *

Republic of the Philippines
Eulogio "Amang" Rodriguez
Institute of Science and Technology
Nagtahan, Sampaloc, Manila

Mrs. Margarita V. Hamada
Founder-Director, Harvent School
Dagupan City

Dear Mrs. Hamada:

Thank you for your article "It Can't Be Done" in the *Manila Bulletin* of Tuesday, 14 July 1987.

I am not as skeptical as your EVP "prophet of doom" who said that your evolutionary teaching technology "can't be done." As an educator, I have always maintained the view of open-mindedness in matters of teaching technology.

While I am writing you personally and entirely on my own without committing the authority of my office nor the Institute, I am prepared to help initiate, should you agree, the establishment of a demonstration school in EARIST.

But I need more facts. Please send me anything I can read about your evolutionary teaching technology. If need be, I am willing to drive all the way to Dagupan to meet and confer with you one of these days; that is, if my proposals are not being taken as too presumptuous.

Very truly yours,

Salvador P. Pascua
Administrative Officer

* * *

Palanan, Makati
5 February 1988

Dear Ms. Hamada:

I'm a practicing pediatrician. Somehow it is not a very self-fulfilling experience lately. Something is very wrong or lacking.

I could not figure it out until I read your enlightening article in the *Manila Bulletin*—"It Can't Be Done!"

I've realized that my real passion is teaching small kids. After reading the article, I felt I had to be a part of that joyful, evolutionary teaching experience. I will be forever grateful if you will give me that opportunity.

Thank you for your kind consideration.

Sincerely yours,

Ma. Nida Sison-Mortero

Sibul, San Miguel
Bulacan
8 February 1988

Mrs. Margarita V. Hamada
Directress, Harvent School
Lingayen, Pangasinan

Ma'am:

Greetings!
I have read your book SCHOOL MYTHTAKES and I can't help but write you a letter of admiration. Congratulations for having written a very informative book, more so for having founded the Harvent School.

I am a new teacher in the public school (I taught kindergarten in a private school last year), the so-called traditional school; am I to be called a traditional teacher, too? How I wish your ideas would be accepted by the higher-ups so as to renovate the present trends in education which I think are mis-education. I myself have some biases and doubts about the present educational system but I have to conform with it because it's my only source of income and I think it's something that nobody can do anything about or maybe I don't have the guts and I'm alone. I envy your teachers who are of great service to your pupils and relieved of all the paper work teachers like us must do. Before, I was thinking how a normal teacher can teach and enjoy at the same time. I thought that was hypothetical, but having read your book, I found out it's real in Harvent School.

Again, congrats, and you have to bear with my penmanship—we do not have a typewriter. By the way, why did you name your school "Harvent School"?

Your new fan,

Vivian A. San Pedro

* * *

Early Learning Center
27 Tampingco St., San Lorenzo Village
Makati, Metro Manila

2 March 1988

Ms. Margarita Ventenilla-Hamada
Harvent School
Dagupan City

Dear Ms. Hamada:

One of the more popular books in our teachers' library is your book, SCHOOL MYTHTAKES. We tend to agree with many of your observations on how children learn. What we would like to happen now is to meet you personally. And this might be possible.

My teachers (about 13 of them) and our four outreach free preschools will be holding an out-of-town evaluation from 21-24 March. We will hold this in Dagupan itself. We hope we can meet with you and see your school on a scheduled date, which is on 22 March, Tuesday, in the afternoon, or the 23rd, if this is convenient for you.

I look forward to hearing from you!
With best wishes!

Yours truly,

Cristina Lim-Yuson, Ph.D.
Directress, ELC

* * *

74

Department of Agricultural Education and Rural Studies
University of the Philippines at Los Baños
College, Laguna, Philippines
29 February 1988

Mrs. Margarita Ventenilla Hamada
Harvent School
Lingayen, Pangasinan

Dear Mrs. Hamada:

I just read your SCHOOL MYTHTAKES and thought of writing to let you know how much I admire your courage, singlemindedness and innovativeness. Your book is a bold indictment of our educational system and the way it is conceptualized. I really think we are missing the boat.

I agree with you that how we define and operationalize learning is the most crucial point. There are a lot of things that I agree with in your book and I wish more people think the same way. You know, you have confirmed my own fears and skepticism about education and I keep asking: is it worth it? Formal education, with all its humiliating and degrading effects on those who "do not make the grade," turns off a lot of talent. I just hope your book gets read by those people who think they know everything about "education" and yet do not cause learning to result from their teaching. Especially the math teachers.

A friend of mine, Dr. J.B. Valera, who got as much stimulation from your book as I did, and I are planning to see your school in the near future to complete our picture of your effort.

I am definitely going to require my students in curriculum development to read your book next semester.

With best wishes,

Higino A. Ables
Professor

* * *

College of Arts and Letters
Department of English and Comparative Literature
University of the Philippines System
Quezon City
7 October 1988

Mrs. Margarita V. Hamada
Directress, Harvent School
Lingayen, Pangasinan

Dear Mrs. Hamada:

Your book, SCHOOL MYTHTAKES, is a breath of fresh air in our congested educational milieu. I bought a copy myself and I want to let you know that I read it with deep interest and satisfaction. I myself have been disappointed with the present system that has been turning out, year in and year out, thousands of graduates—yet our social evils are worse than ever. There is something very wrong with the educational system and you have done something concrete about it. I think your school is the nucleus of the educational approach of the future. Please go on with the good work.

I have been teaching for almost twenty years and I can tell you for a fact that the maladies you talk about in your book are very real. Never before has UP experienced a generation of "grade-conscious" students. At the same time, there is rampant cheating here. In PGH it is worse. The insanity of grades, competition, honors have led to selfishness, exploitation, corruption, and even one suicide last month. UP since its founding has come up with so many summa cum laudes, but look at the list. Do you see any outstanding name among them that has contributed to lead us out of poverty, crime, and wars? None.

I am very interested in your school. I wish you could put up more branches in the future, before the present system strangles us all. May I possibly visit your school and interview you on your philosophy of education for possible publication in a quarterly on education?

Yours very sincerely,

Carlos Ojeda Aureus

* * *

University of the Philippines Los Baños
College, Laguna, Philippines
16 January 1989

Mrs. Margarita V. Hamada
Directress, Harvent School
Lingayen, Pangasinan

Madam:

We, graduate students of UPLB who are taking AERS 220 (Sociology of Education) under Dr. Pura T. Depositario, have heard about your school and are interested in knowing more about it, particularly about the staff, the pupils, methods of instruction, and your views on the teaching-learning process.

We have decided to visit your school on 27 January 1989. The group, which consists of 14 persons including our professor, will be arriving at your school in the afternoon of the same date. We will appreciate it very much if you can extend us your cooperation to make our visit a successful one.

Very truly yours,

Wenifredo T. Onate
Coordinator, AERS 220 students

Noted:

Pura T. Depositario
Professor-in-Charge

* * *

77

Camia Residence Hall
UP Diliman
Quezon City
16 February 1989

Dear Mrs. Hamada:

Presently a BS Biology student in UP Diliman, I will be shifting to BS Family Life and Child Development with one dream in my mind: setting up my own school. Like you, grade school ruined my enthusiasm for school. This isn't a childhood dream (I wanted to become a doctor), but after rummaging through the library, I am certain of the kind of school I'd like to build—one like Harvent School.

Certain doubts are in my mind. I'm too young. There's so much competition. Etcetera. Luckily, I got hold of a copy of your book, and SCHOOL MYTHTAKES (though I haven't read it yet from cover to cover) erased some doubts in my mind. It is with curiosity, appreciation, and admiration that I am writing to you now.

I'm planning to set it up in Olongapo City, my birthplace. But knowing so little, maybe you can send me brochures, pictures of your school, or anything else, for I am finding your project so interesting.

I'm really glad to have read your book!

Sincerely,

Minerva M. Ladores

* * *

San Fernando, La Union
16 March 1989

Dear Mrs. Margarita V. Hamada:

I'm writing you informally now as I feel like a "kindred" spirit with you after reading SCHOOL MYTHTAKES three times. I've been a victim of this so-called traditional educational system and although I've always been top of my class and graduated valedictorian, I always felt I didn't learn anything. (In fact, all my gold medals were lost because I didn't care for them and all my diplomas were hidden.) It was as if I was embarrassed to tell the world about my scholastic achievements. For me they were only scraps of paper that signify pressures and stresses from which I would like to be free forever. I set out to enjoy college life at my own pace. Such attitude shocked my parents.

I'm still very much interested in your concept of school. In fact, I would like to enroll my daughter (5 years old) in your school . I for one would like to teach in such a school. I was not able to pursue such interest as my health did not permit me to.

Very truly yours,

Ma. Nida Sison-Mortero, M.D.

* * *

La Consolacion College
Bacolod City
24 May 1989

Mrs. Margarita V. Hamada
Harvent School
Lingayen, Pangasinan

Dear Mrs. Hamada:

I have read your book, SCHOOL MYTHTAKES, and I got curiously interested in the system you are implementing in your Harvent School. Most of your ideas about school and education reinforced my own beliefs and it will be my personal pride to be able to organize an educational trip to your school and to be treated to a forum with you.

We are a group of elementary and high school teachers from La Consolacion College, Bacolod City, and we intend to visit you and your school sometime in January 1990, God willing.

I hope our plan is agreeable to you. Would you please provide us with useful information regarding this proposed trip?

Thank you for your prompt attention.

Very truly yours,

Mrs. Jona A. Baradero
Area Chairman
Level II Communication Arts Eng./Fil.

28 San Jose, Dasmariñas
414 Cavite
20 July 1989

Mrs. Margarita V. Hamada
Harvent School
Lingayen, Pangasinan

Dear Mrs. M.V. Hamada:

I am Neph J. Sico, a preacher of the gospel. My wife, Evelyn, is a B.S. Psychology graduate who teaches in the Elementary Department of the Philippine Christian University in Dasmariñas.

I have just read some photocopy parts of your amazing book, SCHOOL MYTHTAKES. Sad to say, my friend said it's not available now.

I am interested in this kind of school. Your idea is good. I'd like to know more. Do you have a school like this in our vicinity? Or how can we start one here? We are concerned parents, too. I wish for a wider circulation of your book.

Yours,

Neph J. Sico

Some of My Elementary Graduates Speak

I AM NINE YEARS OLD, and I am through with my Basic Education. If my parents hadn't enrolled me in Harvent School, I would just be in Grade IV this coming June because of the emphasis of the traditional system of education on the class, not on the individual pupil. But because Harvent School is a school that recognizes individual abilities, I did not have to go through the elementary curriculum in six or seven years but in only three years. I learned all the necessary skills in school, not at home, and applied them by reading and writing at my leisure. Now, I am ready to face a high school education, and even the world. My basic skills enabled me to easily win a scholarship in a special Science High School in Dagupan City, where I hope they will be further reinforced, and not submerged in drifts of inert information.

Thank you for sharing my success this afternoon, and wish me more success in the coming years. Thank you.

(Roscor Joy L. Manaois, age 9)

* * *

I am Julius Arenas, and I am 15 years old. You might think that I'm a high school graduate because of my age and height, but I'm not. Let me explain to you why I am graduating from the elementary only now. Well, I was 10 years old when my mother enrolled me in Harvent School. She pulled me out from my former school when she found out that I could not read and write despite three years' stay in that school. Worse, she sensed that I had no interest in learning nor any respect for responsibilities.

When I got accepted in Harvent School, I began to like learning a little bit, because it was presented to me like a game I could play. I was given all the chance to play in school and I was not scolded for loving play above my lessons. The years went by so fast.

Suddenly, reading and working on my lessons became a part of me that I can't remember anymore the unpleasant fact that once upon a time I was a problem boy. If only I did not grow so fast physically, I'd want to stay in school longer. But to do so would give the impression that I'm a slow learner, which I am not. All pupils in elementary schools spend at least six years in the grades; I spent only four years to finish grades one to six, because I spent two years mastering the foundation upon which the skills in the grades are built.

So, my graduating today at age 15 when I enrolled only five years ago speaks well of me as a learner. Had my parents enrolled me in Harvent when I was five, I would have graduated at age 10 or 11, like several of my co-graduates here—but no regrets. Better late than never. After all, I still am lucky to have had six years of the Harvent experience. Thank you and good day to all of you.

(Julius S. Arenas, age 15)

* * *

My mother sees to it that Harvent School provides the best for us. She wants our schooling to be just a sort of leisure rather than an obligation.

Absence of school requirements like homework gave me time to play with my doves and realize at age 11 that I have a bent for veterinary science. This is significant because so many graduates choose the wrong course due to the sad fact that their heavy schoolwork prevented them from playing and picking up a hobby. The result is they do not know what talents they have and what they enjoy doing most.

Successful people in life are not always professionals. In fact, my mother always says that professionals are poor people. The rich people are hobbyists who discovered their hobbies long before their schools robbed them of this chance to do so, because they skipped school after learning the basics. For doing what they enjoyed doing, life has rewarded them with fame and fortune.

I hope that Harvent School's way of developing the skills in me without robbing me of the time for my hobby has started me on the right foot towards success.

I thank you.

(Virgil Anthony V. Hamada, age 11)

* * *

82

One thing I want to share with you all this afternoon is the happy fact that I never developed nervousness and anxiety while going to school. This is because I was personally helped to master the skills listed in the elementary curriculum. I was given exams only after I had finished the skills contained in those exams. Thus getting almost no errors in my exams became a habit to me. There is one thing I never experienced—failing in exams. Even the MECS' surprise exam in 1984 resulted in our getting top scores. The MECS officials were surprised, but not Mrs. Hamada and our teachers at Harvent. Why should they be? They had laid the foundation well for us to hurdle any exam for elementary pupils.

For this, I would like to congratulate my parents for sending me to Harvent School. Thank you.

(Grace Cruz, age 11)

* * *

I don't know what grade I was in for the past years. When I asked my teachers or Mrs. Hamada, they answered there are no grade levels. Nobody is Grade 1, nobody is Grade 2, etc. We are all graders. I felt odd because my friends and neighbors were either Grade 1 or Grade 2 then. Now I discovered why this was so. I came to learn that I finished Nursery, Kinder, Prep and Grades 1 to 7 faster than it would take me if I enrolled in another school. I finished three years of pre-school in two years and Grades 1-7 in only four years.

Now, when anyone asks me what grade I am, I proudly answer that I am an elementary graduate of Harvent School, eager and confident to enter any high school in the world.

(Mark Soriano, age 11)

83

20

Learning Mythtakes

by Carlos Ojeda Aureus

(From "Bookworm," a regular book review column
in *Parents Magazine*, Vol. 11, No. 4, July-August, 1989.)

HARVENT SCHOOL IS DIFFERENT. It has no examinations, no assignments, no grades, no competition among its pupils. In this school, students are advised to read leisurely out of curiosity and not out of pressure, and to spend more time outside the classroom than inside. In a word, Harvent students are advised not to study hard; they're asked to have fun.

This may seem like an invitation to disaster or, at most, an experiment in creating a special school for special students. Neither is true. Harvent School is neither an anarchist's paradise nor a clinic. It's a duly registered school open to everyone, just like any other school recognized by the government.

But there's a difference. In Harvent, unlike other schools, students hate vacations and love going to school.

Indeed, the strangest thing is that in this school, where no one is compelled to come every day, where the catchwords are leisure, free time, and fun, pupils come every day and behave in a way that is all but anarchic. The strangest thing is that students from this school have been getting top scores in the MECS Regional tests, even without reviewing for them!

What is wrong—or right—about this school?

SCHOOL MYTHTAKES is a book about Harvent, a school that is quite different from most others. It tells of an educator who was so dissatisfied with her own schooling that she decided to do something about it "to spare my children the ordeal of having to go through the same experiences I underwent as a student." This educator is MARGARITA VENTENILLA HAMADA, founder and directress of

84

Harvent. She is also the author of the book.

Ms. Hamada does three things in her book:

First, she takes a long, hard look at education today and pits it against the original meaning of school. The Greek word "skole" she reminds us meant leisure, and the English word which derives from the Latin "schola" also meant the same thing. "The origin of education in the liberal arts tradition is not in work, but play," she quotes Conrad Hyers in his essay "The Noblest Game." Learning and leisure are twins: Education is a leisure-time activity. The original meaning of the word "study" in Latin is zeal, and it is zeal for learning she is interested in, not studiousness or training for employment.

The spirit of play is essential to learning. That's what she strives to develop among her students.

Second, she probes into the myths of present-day education, puncturing them like balloons. They're the sort of ideas that can only be held by charlatans, she says, and "charlatans" is exactly how she calls most present-day educators.

Samples of her myths and facts:

Myth: Homework is an aid to learning.
Fact: Homework is an obstable to learning.

Myth: A studious pupil is a promising pupil.
Fact: A studious pupil is a dull pupil.

Myth: Quiz bees promote learning.
Fact: Quiz bees promote knowledge of facts only.

Myth: English is mastered through repeated drills on grammar.
Fact: English is mastered by leisurely reading outside the classroom.

Myth: Well-rounded pupils are estimable.
Fact: Well-rounded pupils don't exist.

Myth: Report cards are pieces of paper on which the competence and incompetence of pupils are recorded.
Fact: Report cards are the pupils themselves showing the competence or incompetence of teachers.

Myth: School helps students keep in step with progress.
Fact: "Half of what we learn in medical or engineering school is obsolete in less than ten years." (Richard Magagna)

These examples are buttressed by biographies, cases, and sayings by great men down the centuries on the subject of education.

Schools like Ateneo de Manila, De la Salle and Maryknoll are, she says, top schools only because their students have very high IQs. But their glory is tarnished by the fact that they choose their students. By doing so, they publicly admit that they can teach only one kind of learner—the fast one. The glory should belong to a school that can teach all kinds of learners effectively.

Third, Hamada presents an alternative, a quite radical philosophy of education which, she claims, has been practiced successfully in her school. Harvent is there to prove to skeptics it can be done.

Harvent first opened in Lingayen, Pangasinan, in 1978, and subsequently set up a branch in Dagupan City. It now counts 275 pupils under its wings. Since its founding, Hamada says, it has touched the lives of about 2000 pupils. Harvent stands for Hamada-Arcinue-Ventenilla. Arcinue is Belle, her sister, and Ventenilla is her brother, Bong. All their children are in Harvent.

Perhaps what ultimately makes Harvent different from most schools is its focus on the individual needs and capacities of its pupils. According to Sister Mary Bellarmine Bernas, OSB (president of St. Scholastica's College, Manila), everything about it—its curriculum, methodology, structure, policies, activities, setting, etc.—was shaped and designed to support the principle that children learn best if allowed to proceed at their own pace.

One of Hamada's favorite stories to show what modern education is doing to our kids is the myth of Procrustes. Procrustes or the Stretcher was an evil-doer who had an iron bedstead upon which he tied his victims. If they were longer than the bed, he would cut off as much as was necessary. If they were shorter, he would stretch their limbs until they were long enough to fit the bed. (See *Parents*, Vol. 11, No. 5, May-June 1989, p. 34. Ed.)

Modern education is due for an overhaul, Hamada asserts. Despite the PhD's, MBA's, MD's and MA's we produce year in and year out, our society is not getting any better. What is wrong with the way we train our students? Great numbers of our youth go to school yearly, and yet school has failed to lead us out of poverty, graft and corruption. Students lie, cheat, and even commit suicide under extreme pressure by a system that does not even deliver.

Maybe it's time we tied Procrustes to his own bed?

Part Two

RELIGION, MARRIAGE, SOCIAL WORK, ETC.

*"None may arrive at the Truth
until he is able to think that the Path
itself may be wrong."*
—Idries Shah

21

Believing—the Wrong Road
to Truth and Progress; or
The Dangers of Freezing the Mind

HOWEVER ERRONEOUS AND INEFFECTIVE the American public school system is, it has one redeeming factor to its credit, to the benefit of education and mankind in general: It does not allow the public schools to teach religion.

The reason could have been the not-so-dim memory of the horrors of religious inquisitions the Founding Fathers had fled from in the Old World. Not wanting to have bloody history repeat itself in the New World they were then trying to establish, they banned religion from the classroom. That singular act, inspired by their "anti-theological" American Constitution, led to the America we gape at in awe today: progressive spiritually and materially. Which just goes to show that true spirituality need not come from religion.

What Is Religion?

What is religion? Why has it hounded mankind since time immemorial? How come more evil than good is associated with it? How come great thinkers who have done mankind the most good (Albert Einstein, Bertrand Russell, Francis Bacon, Ayn Rand, Ralph Waldo Emerson, George Bernard Shaw, Arnold Toynbee, Ikeda) do not belong to any religious sect even if they are aware of and do not deny the existence of an Absolute Power? How come history's great butchers like Mahomet, Hitler, Bishop Jim Jones (of the Guyana massacre), Queens Mary and Elizabeth I, Cardinal Richilieu, Joan of Arc and Charlemagne were religious fanatics?

The dictionary defines religion as "Belief in superhuman-controlling power especially of a personal God or gods entitled to obedience and worship."

Ikeda, a historian and a respected mind from Japan, thinks religion is "reverence for the ultimate reality transcending human knowledge which makes possible ethical behavior."

But what is this ultimate reality which sustains all knowledge? Does religion which has so far monopolized this territory really know what it is? How does it "know" this Absolute? Does it have a perfect language to describe the Perfection it purports to lead us to?

Does Religion Lead or Mislead?

Let me answer my own questions. The fact that there are so many religions in the world means religion does not know this ultimate reality. It can only hazard guesses based on inherited fossils of superstitions from ignorant persons made eminent by antiquity. Because, were the fact about the Absolute known, there would be no need for other religions to spring up and give their versions to further confuse the world. Religion cannot explain this ultimate reality because it sees NOTHING. It sees nothing because it does not investigate but merely depends on the revelations of authorities—authorities in the form of fallible men called prophets and high priests and their "sacred" books containing the doctrines they believe in.

Belief. This is the stuff which religion is entirely made up of—"a shortcut to knowledge, which is only a short circuit destroying the mind" (Nathaniel Branden in *The Virtue of Selfishness*). Beliefs are opinions, and "opinions distort your senses if they are just the ones that suit you." (Idries Shah, *Thinkers of the East*). "Beliefs obscure and distort reality; they do not reveal it. We cannot see anything outside of a belief." (Willard and Marguerite Beecher, *Beyond Success and Failure*). Because religion repudiates any reality outside its prison cell of beliefs on the illusion that it already "knows," Emerson says, "Religion effeminates and demoralizes."

The Beginnings of Religion

Religion has its origin in man's feeling that he is not independent, that there are superior forces beyond his control and that the Absolute of these forces sustains life. Naturally, he wants to commune and be in harmony with this unmanifest Absolute. Thus, Religion started from man's feelings of inferiority. But here is something interesting: Man began to feel inferior only after his banishment from Eden.

When Adam and Eve lived in Eden, there was no religion on earth. They lived in complete harmony with its laws of nature. They talked with, not worshipped, the Absolute. Their life was a life of bliss. All their needs were provided for by nature. Because all their thoughts, words and actions were spontaneously right, nature gave them full support.

But then—they ate the fruit of the tree of knowledge of good and evil, and disaster struck. Their harmony with nature was broken. They suddenly became outsiders—inferiors, no longer peers—to that Absolute they hid from and whom they now must look up to for the support they desired. With harmony now broken, life suddenly became a struggle.

The forbidden fruit that they ate is religion. It enlightened them to see good and evil and so evil became a part of their life. It became a reality—that is to say, religion made sin a living reality by naming what sin is. Thus, the first murder on earth occurred shortly after religion became a part of man's lifestyle.

The Many Evils of Religion

Cain slew his brother Abel because he worshipped differently from him. This means they were not alike, and "from the beginning of history, observed James Michener in *Hawaii*, "people who are not alike have hated one another." Abel offered the firstlings of his flock. Cain offered the fruits of his orchard. God preferred Abel's animals to Cain's fruits, so Abel's kind of worship was BETTER than Cain's. Comparison. Disparity. Competition. Bigotry.

"Mine is true. Yours is false. You are ugly. I am beautiful. That is cheap. This is class." Conflicts began, resulting in persecution and death. From that first single murder whose cause was religious worship, the statistics have squared and cubed. The world has become hell, its flames fanned by religion. Human beings were slaughtered by priests with the approval of the people in religious ceremonies. Abraham, whom the Jews revere as their foremost patriarch, was willing to murder his only son, Isaac, to propitiate his God. His action (which we civilized human beings today would heavily penalize with the electric chair) has been highly endorsed by religious leaders who keep re-telling the story to the younger generations. Agamemnon sacrificed his own daughter to buy a favor from Poseidon, for which Lucretius the poet was quoted by Francis Bacon to have said, "To such ill actions Religion could persuade a man."

Throughout history, men who sought to know nature and the workings of our universe have been persecuted and murdered by religion.

An early victim of religious bigotry was Socrates, a great thinker and teacher, who lived and taught the youth in ancient Greece. He was executed by the Greek religious leaders because he denied the existence of the gods officially recognized in Greece: Zeus, Apollo, etc., thereby "corrupting the minds of the youth." What they didn't say was the truth—that they were afraid and angry that a thinker could endanger their position of eminence they had easily achieved by blindfolding the public.

The most famous victim of religious bigotry was Jesus Christ (although most of the Roman Catholics have not realized it yet because they do not read the whole story of Christ's life but content themselves with parts and parcels of the whole from the Vatican). His death was orchestrated by the Pharisees and the Sadducees, the Jewish religious leaders, because he taught different things from what they had been teaching for ages. Whereas they taught of a wrathful, vengeful God, Christ spoke of a loving, forgiving Father in Heaven. Where they preached hatred for Gentiles, Publicans and Samaritans, He taught love for all, and so He was crucified for daring to point out the goodness in nature.

Joan of Arc, a very religious maid of Orleans, France, who led the French to battle (yes, she led to kill) and to victory against the English, did not die from the hands of the enemy. She died because the jealous French clergy sold her to the English, who accused her of heresy and witchcraft and manipulated the proceedings so she would get the death penalty. She was thus burned at the stake. What is funny about her case is that the same church that condemned her in 1430 canonized her in 1919.

This same fear and blind fury rooted in religion led to the persecution and holocaust of the Jews, a very "religious" but different race from Hitler's idea of the superior race just a generation or two ago.

The next evil associated with religion aside from the obvious persecutions and murder of good men and women is the less obvious, but more dangerous, resistance it puts up against new truths and discoveries that lead to progress. To religious bigots, "ignorances, habits, beliefs and passions are dearer than happiness, progress or even life," notes Bertrand Russell. Krishnamurti bitterly resents the historical fact that "all organized religions have been the bane of civilization." Eric Von Daniken, in *The Gold of the Gods,* is convinced that "religions with their countless gods hinder progress," and that "if their insight does not improve, they will be a contributing cause of the end of human existence."

Consider the following facts from history so that these denouncements of religion by great thinkers can be better understood:

A great scientist, Galileo, was punished with house arrest until his death by the Catholic Church for publishing his scientific discovery that conflicted with what the Church was teaching. At that time, the Church taught a very unscientific and therefore false dogma—that the earth is the center of the universe because it is the home of man who was created according to God's image. Galileo's finding after much careful study was that the earth is not the center of the universe. It is just an ordinary planet among seven or eight others circling the sun. For daring to refute their teachings with a fact, the Church authorities made Galileo's life miserable.

When Benjamin Franklin invented the lightning rod, thereby removing a very real terror from man's life, he was denounced from the pulpit as a wicked man who dared to "interfere with God's justice." At that time, it was believed that God used lightning to strike at sinners. This instance shows that Religion which was founded to help the progress of the human soul has ironically become its prison.

When the compass was invented, religionists who could not explain how it worked, raised a furor about it. They believed its power came from the devil and forbade their fellow-believers from using it, thereby delaying the progress of navigation for many centuries. This was true also with the radio and the tape recorder. Only when science came out with the explanation that the compass and then much later, the radio and then the tape recorder's power came from a force called electromagnetism, and not from the devil, did the furor die down. Now, these religionists use these inventions they had fearfully denounced in the past to further perpetuate their goals against progress.

All these religious persecutions so well recorded by history must have somehow saved another great thinker from the same fate at the hands of the Catholic Church. The Church had learned a lesson from its condemnation of Galileo in the past. It had lost face when the man it condemned was vindicated by science to have said the truth, so when another Galileo sprang up in the person of one of its priests, Pierre Teilhard de Chardin (a great grand nephew of Voltaire), the Church did not condemn him this time but issued, instead, a monitum of the Holy Office in 1962 which merely warned against uncritical acceptance of his theories. Chardin's mind worked towards uniting religion and science so that he could decipher man's role in the universe. He knew that religion alone, without the help of science, could not reveal what he desperately sought, so he dared to probe reality with science. For daring to do such a thing—THINK AND RESEARCH—he was considered a dangerous innovator and was "saved from ecclesiastical condemnation by his good faith alone."

Everyone desires a life of health, happiness and prosperity," says Brian Adams in his book *How to Succeed*, "yet few succeed in experiencing those affirmative states because of false beliefs and the misus of their thinking powers."

Thus has world peace become an elusive goal because of religion. The bloodshed and the horrors of religious wars must have been known to Francis Bacon, for he enunciated this truth: "The quarrels and divisions about religion were evils unknown to the heathen." Early Christians were fed to the lions by the powerful Romans who refused to recognize Christ as Son of God. They insisted Jupiter had no such son. Muslims, faithfully obeying their prophet, Mahomet, paid their way to salvation by killing infidels—those who hold different beliefs. The Crusaders (militant Christians) retaliated. With the Holy Cross as their battle insignia, they killed the Saracens in the name of God. Later, when Christianity flourished, petty differences within the Christian dogmas resulted in a bitter, continuing conflict between Roman Catholics and Protestants. In England, Henry VIII beheaded the Catholics (two of them, Sir Thomas More and Sir Edmund Campion) who refused to recognize him as the head of the Anglican Church which he founded as an act of defiance to the Catholic Church's Infallible Pope who refused him a divorce from his Roman Catholic wife, Catherine of Aragon. When he died, Queen Mary, his daughter by Catherine of Aragon, put to death non-Catholics. She is known as Bloody Mary in history. When Mary died, her half-sister, Elizabeth I, daughter of Anne Boleyn, beheaded Catholics, thus continuing the bloodbath begun by her predecessor not a few years back.

Everywhere, members of different religious sects keep criticizing and insulting each other's beliefs: "We are Roman Catholics. Our Pope is infallible! Our religion was founded by Jesus Christ who is God, not by men or prophets who founded your religions." Jews and Christians have forgotten and even deny their common roots, in their never-ending wranglings about religion: "You are marrying a Protestant? She will insult our Jewish home with a Christmas tree!" "Well, don't force her to attend our Hanukka so she won't also force her Christian beliefs on us!" Asians are also divided because of different beliefs. "We Muslims are the only ones who know the truth. We don't believe in the Trinity because there is only one God." "We Hindus don't worship any personality. We prefer the real forces, not deities." "We Chinese worship our dead ancestors, not gods." "We Buddhists don't pray for anything lest we be frustrated. We rid our hearts of all desires instead."

Alas, because of all these conflicts, Napoleon Hill, America's leading exponent of prosperity, speaks facetiously but rightfully against religion: "It is a major indictment against the religionists that they seem to have learned so much about how to prepare to live in Heaven—but have done so little about preparing us to live prosperously, peacably, and happily, here, now."

Finally, it is significant that the new evil religion called Communism was born in the heart of Christendom. A Jehovah's Witness publication, *What Has Religion Done for Mankind?*, in attempting to show that its dogma is the true one, brings to our attention that "the lands where Communism has its strongholds and its greatest number of adherents are lands where there has been union of Church and State and where religious hierarchies have dominated the lives and politics of the people, such as Russia, Italy, France, etc."

So Ayn Rand's observation that "every dictator is a mystic and every mystic is a potential dictator" is true. Both demand surrender of their subjects'/parishioners' mind—and that the Church (mystic) and State (dictator) are "implacable enemies of both intelligence and virtue" as succinctly put by Bertrand Russell.

Religion Is the Wrong Road to Truth

"The sacred books tell you what you should do and what you should not do. Why do you accept the propaganda of churches or politicians?" Krishnamurti asks this impossible question, knowing we cannot answer it. We cannot answer it because our minds have been habituated into believing "authorities," and not into thinking for ourselves. Very few people have done so and they are the few great minds this world has ever produced. Hermann Hesse, in his best-loved bestseller *Siddharta,* proudly says he is a thinker: "I have become distrustful of teachings and learning and I have little faith in words that come to us from teachers." Ralph Waldo Emerson, my favorite thinker, in his essay "Worship," is also proud of the fact that he uses his mind. "No facts are to me sacred, none are profane; I simply experiment, an endless seeker with no Past at my back. Why should we import rags and relics into the new hour? We have another sight, a new standard, an ear which hears not what men say, but hears what they do not say." George Bernard Shaw, the rival of Emerson in my list of favorite minds, thinks that believing has a saturation point in us, and that will be the time, he enthuses, that the products of a better mental process called thinking, will come into our lives: "When we refuse to believe in the miracles of religion for no better reason fundamentally than that we are no longer in the humor for them we refill our minds with the miracles of science, most of which the authors of the Bible would have refused to believe." Religionists, as has been proven in these pages, are not thinkers, but believers. Taylor Caldwell warns us in her novel *Bright Flows the River* that "they are trained to explain the inexplicable so they use dogma and cant which soothe but clarify nothing." This is because "it is a fact that the most religious men are not the most intelligent," so Bertrand Russell boldly states his observation, adding, "It is a well-known fact that the professional moralist in our day is a man of less than average intelligence."

Because religion's very nature is anti-intellectual, it can never lead people to the truth. It can only deceive and temporarily pacify the great masses of people "who might otherwise be rebelling in the streets against the injustices of life on earth," says author Gay Talese. And because it can not lead us to the Truth, it can not also lift us above suffering, because the twin of ignorance is suffering.

Knowing this, we are now in a better position to decide "whether to accept the authority of the Church or the conclusions of our private judgments as the interpreters of God's will," challenges George Bernard Shaw. And knowing that "the religions of the world are the ejaculations of a few imaginative men," and that "the quality of the imagination is to flow, and not to freeze," points out Emerson, why should we prefer anything above the powers of our own intellect?

Thinking, investigating, challenging existing facts lead to the Truth that maintains man. This process of thinking, including its consequent product—Truth—is scientific technology. "It is so much more advanced a thing than belief," concedes Idries Shah, a thinker from the East, because "those who really know are seven hundred degrees in rank above those who only believe." Science impels all men to think and investigate—to freely question and challenge any prophet, book or belief, to get at the truth. It tests all findings, and turns even the most sacred belief into dust in its process of seeking. It believes nothing and therefore does not presume to know. And, most important, unlike religion which detests anything new and different, science opens itself to newer findings and corrects previous theories that stood on some error. Science, being an independent discipline, not a belief dependent on the authority of a prophet, can never veer from the Truth for selfish reasons. It has no interest or purpose but to pursue, to find the answer—and to explain and share the secret it sees with its powerful eyes. The eyes of Science are powerful because they are not veiled by the mists of beliefs (which are mere suppositions) that are being upheld as truth by religionists who lack the proper instruments and the attitude of unknowingness from whence all truth springs.

Because the eyes of Science are clear and unobstructed, its language is precise, its truth is the truth. There could be no confusion about it. Hence, Peace results and shall abide—only as long as Reality stays in the language of Science. When Science is lost, Truth is lost. Religion will spring up as its poor, nay, dangerous, substitute, attempting to teach what it can never see nor fathom, leading its believers into a life of suffering and endless strife.

Modern science, especially Quantum Physics, has recently opened the door to the Absolute with the discovery of the Unified Field for which Abdus Salam, Steven Weinberg, and Sheldon Glashow won the Nobel Peace Prize for Physics in 1979. The mathematical equations and the precise language of physics have now brought this beautiful Truth into our life—nothing in life is any longer mysterious. All can be explained. Against this Truth unearthed by science- how can poor, intuitive religionists disagree?

So, our philosophy for progress should be that of Robert S. de Ropp (author of *The Master Game*): "Have faith in nothing. Believe in nothing. Test everything." And our prayer should be Anjin San's prayer in James Clavell's *Shogun*: "God, protect me from wounds and all doctors. And priests."

The Only Road to Truth

A passage from the powerful book *Uncle Tom's Cabin* by Harriet Beecher Stowe goes this way:

> Religion! Is what you hear at church religion? Is that which can bend and turn and descend and ascend, to fit every crooked phase of selfish, worldly society, religion? Is that religion which is less scrupulous, less generous, less just, less considerate for man, than even my own ungodly, worldly, blinded nature? No! When I look for a religion, I must look for something above me, and not something beneath.

This quest for the ideal road to truth, which is the opposite of religion, has been the dominant thought in many great thinkers' minds:

"My faith is a mosaic of unbelief," says Zorba, in Nikos Kazantzakis' novel, *Zorba the Greek*. "Fierce beliefs. They died for them. I don't think they were worth dying for. I don't think any belief is worth dying for. Do I? Maybe I'll find one that is. Then it will be worth living for, too," declared Anna Friedman, main protagonist in Belva Plain's bestseller, *Evergreen*. "One believes in God, piously going to church. Another believes as deeply, without Church, but in loving his fellow man," points our Jess Sterne, in his book *The Power of Alpha Thinking*. And as usual, Emerson shares another of his majestic thoughts in describing the ideal road to truth. He says, "God builds his temple in the heart, on the ruins of churches and religions." Ikeda's concept of this ideal road is a religion based on a law, not on a god, because he says, "Such a religion is not only faithful to, but also surpasses modern ideas of logicality and reason." Arnold Toynbee thinks the ideal road is more of "an attitude to life that enables people to cope with the difficulty of being human by giving spiritually satisfying answers to the fundamental questions about the mystery of the universe and of man's role in it and by giving practical precepts for living in the universe." Ikeda is more specific in describing this ideal road:

> It will be able to take the lead in a civilization on a high plane that combines both science and philosophy. It must inspire mankind's scientific and philosophical spirits and must be able to meet the needs of a new age. It must be a religion that can go beyond the differences between East and West and, binding all mankind into a unified body, save the Occident from its present crisis and the Orient from its current hardships. Discovering this (ideal road) is the greatest task before mankind today.

Taylor Caldwell, at age 12, already had the confident vision that this ideal road is somewhere near. She said, "We may yet discover what the Creator is, and how He works! This quest constitutes our religion, and the universe is our church." True enough, she lives to see her optimism manifest itself through recent strides in modern physics. Michael Talbot in his book *Mysticism and the New Physics* tells us in plain words that "the new physics is offering us a scientific basis" for this ideal road. He explains that "the religion offered by the new physics is not a religion of values or absolute principles. It offers us no strict delineation of heavens or hells. It is a religion based on the psychology of the human consciousness—indeed, on the psychology of the entire universe as a conscious force acting upon itself." What Michael Talbot is talking about is the Unified Field which physicists and mathematicians describe as superconsciousness, which is the main switchboard of all the laws of nature running the cosmos, the Absolute in the precise and clear language of physics and mathematics.

Albert Einstein, whom the world considers the greatest mind since Jesus Christ, knew what the Unified Field is all about because he devoted the last years of his life delving into this ultimate basis of matter and creation. Even before he could unlock the secret of this Absolute (he died leaving his quest unfinished), he felt he had already found the ideal road.

When asked what religion he practised, he could not name any of the present religious sects, but here is his answer:

> The most beautiful thing we can experience is the mysterious. To know that what is impenetrable to us really exists, manifesting itself as the highest wisdom and the most radiant beauty which our dull faculties can comprehend only in their most primitive forms—this knowledge, this feeling, is at the center of true religiousness. In this sense, I belong in the ranks of devoutly religious men. (Quoted by Irving Wallace in his novel *The Word*.)

Its Tests

The ideal road to truth is not Religion which merely believes, but Science (its technology, attitude and spirit) which thinks and questions and reasons. The end result of religion is ignorance and its twin sons, suffering and strife, because its basis is superstition. The end result of science is enlightenment and its twin daughters, peace and progress, because its basis is demonstrated truth sired by reason.

The dominant character of religion is fanaticism, which is defined by Irving Wallace as "excess of zeal and, therefore, lack of love."

Science, the ideal road to truth, on the other hand, has only one characteristic that is its final test. It is not religiousness but Love. This means no fear at all to be open about the whole of reality.

If some private schools insist on teaching religion, they must teach all religions, so that their pupils will grow up knowing that there are many interpretations of one reality. From there, they will seek the best. In this way, these schools will be teaching pupils to think and compare, and not to believe in just one facet of reality. The religion they will find will be one of validatable insights, and not of incontestable beliefs. The school will thus stop being the ice-boxes that they are, freezing students' minds. They will become catalysts for the flow of thoughts, which should be their only role. And in enacting this role, they will never forget what all great thinkers knew—Thinking, not believing, is the only way to truth and progress.

22

Pity Is Not Charity

IT NEVER OCCURRED TO ME BEFORE that most of the evil in the world can be traced to pity. After all, my solid Catholic education both at home and in school taught me that it is a virtue, an intrinsic part of the highest one at that—Love. My Catholic elders called it charity, and they defined it as pity for the poor and the weak and the unfortunate. They based their teachings on what Christ said: "Feed the hungry, clothe the naked, visit the sick and the imprisoned, etc."

What Christ had failed to do was to give charity a definite definition, and so Christendom has since floundered in the sticky consequence of mistaken indentity. We thought pity is charity and we were never corrected on our presumption. But like the Prince and the Pauper who looked identical, they are actually different. To have had placed the crown on the pauper's head resulted in near tragedy in that kingdom, so Mark Twain's story goes.

And so it did, with Christendom and the rest of the world. Tragedy has been the result of having persistently confounded these two synonyms (again, there is error in this classification). Because we uphold pity as a virtue, the world is now in the clutches of an evil religion called Communism, whose foundation is Christian charity. Note that the first socialist/communist countries had been the bulwark of Christianity before: Italy (where St. Peter's Basilica is situated in its capital city, Rome), Russia (its capital, Moscow, has the most number of cathedrals in the whole world), Germany, and for a while, under Generalissimo Franco, Spain—the country that Christianized us. Let's not leave out Cuba, a Hispanized Catholicized country, which is now Communism's door to the United States.

Because the United States took pity towards developing nations through dole-outs called foreign aid, the Philippines is now one hundred times poorer than when it was not yet their object of pity. Because a rich family took in a homeless relative into their home out of a sense of Christian charity, they were robbed of domestic peace forever. Because a father took pity on his eldest son for being jobless, he made him manager of his ranches which the son promptly sold as his own. Because a nurse had so kindly sent her fiance to medical school, he married another girl and left her out in the cold. Because a financially independent wife subsidized her husband's projects, their marriage ended on the rocks. Because teachers pity the dull and indifferent students, they consequently flood our society with unemployable graduates. Because the Land Reform Law took pity on the farmers, and gave them lands stolen from their owners, we now have to import rice. (The word stolen is the correct term because no sale is valid without the owner's consent to sell, at his price, not the Land Reform's.) Because the Department of Labor sides with the "poor laborers," unemployment (from the closure of business firms) and inflation have escalated uncontrollably. Because government officials give "ghost" jobs to the pitiful unemployed, our coffers are empty. Democracy has become DemoCRAZY.

Why is it that the hand that gives is always bitten? Why are ingratitude and perdition the curious results of generosity, sometimes called philanthropy? Why is a benefactor usually betrayed and given a slap in the face? The book *The Money Motive* by Thomas Wiseman (London, 1974) has a good explanation: ". . . gratitude is an emotion we are often quite incapable of feeling because it involves the imagined humiliation of feeling small and inadequate in relation to somebody else's bigness and richess."

Why is Social Work the breeding ground of tramps and moochers? Why are public projects for social welfare "mausoleums not always in shape but always in cost" as observed by Ayn Rand? Is charity a crime, and not the virtue we think it is, to spark such negative consequences? You bet it is, if taken and expressed for its counterfeit—pity.

Pity is negative. It is charity's outward shell minus the living entity within. That is why it does not support or nourish but hurts and destroys. "It is a very easy thing to toss a copper to a beggar on the street," says the pamphlet, *The Greatest Thing in the World*; "it is generally an easier thing than not to do it. . . . We purchase relief from the sympathetic feelings roused by the spectacle of misery, at the copper's cost. It is too cheap—too cheap for us and often too dear for the beggar. If we really loved him we would either do more for him, or less, because Love is just as often in the withholding . . ." Harriet Beecher Stowe loved the Negro. Her heart went out to their plight. But she did not spend her life nor her life's savings on helping the fugitive slaves escape from their cruel masters. She did not feed them nor nurse them. She did something more for them: She eradicated slavery from the face of the United States. She used her talents, time, energy and courage in dealing slavery one mortal blow through her book, *Uncle Tom's Cabin*. That book, say historians and social scientists today, was the singular stroke that brought an end to slavery. Who among our social workers can equal the love of Mrs. Stowe? To me, she, not Mother Teresa, should be considered the Saint!

Charity is something alive, a living expression of love and respect for one's fellowmen. "Love," says Ayn Rand, "is an expression and assertion of self-esteem, a response to one's own values in the person of another." Therefore, a person who loves himself loves his fellowmen spontaneously, not out of duty, or out of pity. Without these vital principles—love and respect for others—charity is dead. It becomes a lifeless shell, a sham of what had been vital and nourishing before. It becomes pity.

Charity sees men realistically and loves them for their individual differences and respects them for what they are, be they physically ugly or morally weak or mentally crippled. It knows that withholding alms from them is loving them and respecting them. This kind of love ennobles. It is the force that inspires the lowly and the humble to rise above their lot on their own efforts. Genuine love, not altruistic services, points out Ralph Waldo Emerson, is felt by them and "they don't leave out the holder of that virtue. They delight in him."

But pity refuses to see reality. Where it sees ugliness and incompetence and stupidity, it disrupts nature by "correcting" these with alms and social services. Ayn Rand urges us to note that "the monument to socialism is a pyramid of public factories, public theatres and public parks, erected on a foundation of human corpses" who had bled for the public good. Pity attempts to play God, a despicable crime in itself. It "equalizes" all men and makes them all an anonymous mass of humanity surviving on limited goods distributed equally among them. God did not create all men to be the same. Being a God of infinite variety, He created them to differ in abilities, inclinations, tempers and ambitions. They are equal only in their right to pursue their own happiness, and this they can do without the interference of power-lusters (politicians) whom Ayn Rand described to be intertwined with the public because they "fuel their desire for unearned greatness (which they term 'prestige') with the public—public needs, public projects." The public. The public interest. Service to the public. These, points out Ayn Rand in her book *The Virtue of Selfishness,* are the "means, the tools, the swinging pendulum of the power-luster's self-hypnosis."

Robin Hood, the first communist, lived Christ's teachings to the hilt. With a great show of virtue, he robbed the rich and gave the poor those stolen goods, making banditry honorable and even romantic. (Just like how a rebel priest's similar misguided cause has been romanticized in a movie entitled Balweg!) And mind, his most zealous followers were friars. Which gives me a morsel to chew on: Why is it that the unproductive like Robin Hood and his band (our modern-day Department of Agrarian Reform, the Department of Labor and rebel priests up in the mountains) are the ones bitten by this negative emotion, pity? Is it because they, like this shell, are also dead and empty inside?

Pity does not love or respect the substandard. It confirms it, by condescending to change it. For this absence of love and respect, the very natural result is ingratitude in the form of a slap in the face. Serves anyone right for condescending. Condescension is pity because it is the reverse of respect and admiration. "What a dreadful thing true pity is!" moans Ayn Rand. Margaret Mitchell, in her *Gone with the Wind* seconds this wail, saying, "Pity and contempt always go together." "It kills the soul of him who receives and debauches the one who giveth," puts in the young Taylor Caldwell in her first book, *Atlantis*. "It is not the office of a man to receive gifts. How dare you give them?" chides Emerson in his essay "Gifts" and says further, "We can receive anything from love, for that is a way of receiving it from ourselves, but not from anyone who assumes to bestow. It is a very onerous business, this of being served, and the debtor naturally wishes to give you a slap."

More dramatically, Ayn Rand describes for us this rotting carcass called pity in her famous bestseller, *The Fountainhead:*

> But this was pity—this complete awareness of man without worth or hope, this sense of finality, of the not to be redeemed. There was shame in this feeling—his own shame that he should have to pronounce such judgment upon a man, that he should know an emotion which contained no shred of respect.
>
> This is pity, he thought, and then he lifted his head in wonder. He thought that there must be something terribly wrong with a world in which this monstrous feeling is called a virtue.

The warp and woof of charity, on the other hand, is love and self-respect. "Self-respect is closely bound up with paying one's way," according to the book *The Money Motive*.

Pity supports parasites. Charity supports producers. Pity gives alms, largesse. Charity gives loans and ideas and challenges. Pity supports need. Charity supports ability and integrity. Pity plays God and tries to do what only God can do: It impoverishes the rich so that their poor brothers will have company. Charity accepts God's work, and admires it, not daring to question it and insult the Divine Plan. It does not hurt, deprive or coerce or prevent anyone from pursuing his rightful share of his labors. It helps people help themselves by not robbing them of their dignity through alms. It does not give things for free to undeserving people. By undeserving is meant unvirtuous—devoid of self-respect to pay his way through life. There's really nothing free. We pay for the oxygen we breathe with the carbon dioxide our lungs manufacture. We pay for the fruits we eat by planting and watering our trees and smoking out worms from their boughs and with the carbon dioxide we exhale in the process. We pay for the beauty of nature by cultivating our sense of reverence for it. We pay for our place in this universe by using our talents in productive work.

So, who then do we help? And when do we give anything free?

From Ayn Rand's *The Virtue of Selfishness*, here are guidelines we can follow:

If one's friend is in trouble, one should act to help him by whatever nonsacrificial means are appropriate. For instance, if one's friend is starving, it is not a sacrifice, but an act of integrity to give him money for food rather than buy some insignificant gadget for oneself, because his welfare is important in the scale of one's personal values. If the gadget means more than the friend's suffering, one has no business pretending to be his friend.

And when do we help a stranger? From the same book, we have the following guideline:

It is on the ground of that generalized goodwill and respect for the value of human life that one helps strangers in an emergency —and only in an emergency.

Suppose one hears that the man next door is ill and penniless. Illness and poverty are not metaphysical emergencies, they are part of the normal risks of existence, but since the man is temporarily helpless, one may bring him food and medicine. If one can afford it (as an act of goodwill, not of duty) or one may raise a fund among the neighbors to help him out. But this does not mean that one must support him from then on, nor that one must spend one's life looking for starving men to help. Poverty, ignorance, illness and other problems of that kind are not metaphysical emergencies. By the metaphysical nature of man and of existence, man has to maintain his life by his own effort; the values he needs—such as wealth or knowledge—are not given to him automatically, as a gift of nature, but have to be discovered and achieved by his own thinking and work.

One's sole obligation toward others, in this respect, is to maintain a social system that leaves men free to achieve, to gain and to keep their values.

(Take note, Mother Teresa! Wouldn't it be best for you to devote your energy and good name to changing the social system that produces such poverty your hands cannot cope with, instead of doing those acts of mercy? Dealing with the problem at its source—studying the mechanics of the social system that grinds out so much human dross and changing it will beat whatever attention you give this system's external results.)

Christ's ambiguousness (or is it the Vatican's? After all, it is already an established fact that the Church had scissored off certain chapters from the gospel like the treatise on reincarnation and the documents establishing where Jesus Christ had spent his years from age 13 to 29) deceived us into thinking that charity and pity are the same. Hence all this poverty, wickedness, strife and hopelessness. Perhaps India's poverty can be blamed on their concept of charity—alms-giving and pampering the needy. (In India, most sages or ascetics, or Holy Men, are beggars, whose empty bowls are objects of everyone's charity.) Also the poverty of countries that have been conquered by Catholic Spain—Mexico, Guatemala, Puerto Rico, and most countries in the South American continent. This is no longer something to be wondered at, if we know (as I have recently learned), that, after all, the Hindu philosophy on charity is the basic stuff of Christianity.

Our schools must put the crown back where it rightfully belongs by careful definition of these two words. Schools should warn against pity and should exert efforts to eradicate it from our vocabulary. With it gone, beggars, professional parasites, vagrants will also make their exit. Progress, ushered in by achievers who have love, not pity in their hearts, will take their place. The world will then be suffused with the glow of true holiness, which is another word for integrity, love, and self-respect or all these in just one word—CHARITY.

23

Envy—A Necessary Evil?

ENVY—THAT GREEN GOBLIN. I first met this ugly malefactor when I was seven years old, in the fairy tale "The Sleeping Beauty." It took the form of a fairy named "Maleficent," who, having been accidentally overlooked in the Princess Aurora's christening party gave the said princess a gift of the utmost malevolence—sudden death at age 15 from a prick of the needle of a spinning wheel. It should be noted that the apparent reason given in the story was spite due to a sin of omission by her parents. The real reason dawned on me clearly only today. The hundreds of stories I have since read between that time and now, plus my own observations and experiences, allowed me to glimpse what would otherwise not have been obvious—that her malevolent gift was given not out of spite but out of envy—that green goblin whose green blood poisons, corrodes, and kills the object of its perverted fancy. Please note that the Princess Aurora had been gifted by the good fairies with EVERYTHING—beauty, grace, wisdom, wealth, health, power, privilege, love and adulation. Aside from royalty. Too much Spring. Too fierce the Winter.

The Chinese are painfully aware of this demon's existence. In Pearl S. Buck's *The Good Earth*, Wang Lung and O Lan carefully disguised their joy at their good fortune of having a healthy son by rubbing dirt on the child's face and by loudly lamenting, "But our child is only a poor wretched baby girl—so sickly and worthless!" lest they attract this green goblin's venomous eyes and bring disaster upon their son and themselves.

Yes, immortals get envious, and when they do, woe to the mortal-object of their envy. Edgar Allan Poe expressed the bitter grief of lovers whom envious spirits smote in the following lines from his immortal poem, "Annabel Lee":

> But we loved with a love that was more than love,
> I and my Annabel Lee,

With a love that the winged seraphs of heaven
Coveted her and me.

And this was the reason that long ago,
In this kingdom by the sea,
A wind blew out of a cloud, chilling
My beautiful Annabel Lee;
So that her high-born kinsmen came,
    and bore her away from me,
To shut her up in a sepulchre,
In this kingdom by the sea.

The angels, not half so happy in heaven,
Went envying her and me.
Yes! That was the reason (as all men know)
In this kingdom by the sea,
That the wind came out of the cloud by night
Chilling and killing my Annabel Lee.

See? Exceedingly beautiful women like Annabel Lee who had been favored by fortune with other coveted gifts like nobility of lineage (pedigree), talent, wealth, fame, all put together, had all been struck down with some searing tragedy which offset these gifts. Elegant and beautiful Jacqueline Kennedy, considered by the world media as a real "thoroughbred," was splattered by her husband's blood when an assassin's bullet took his life at the peak of his career as President of the United States. Natalie Wood, personification of haunting beauty, talent, wealth (to a certain degree) and fame, died tragically from accidental drowning. Grace Kelley, daughter of a millionaire, a breathtakingly beautiful and famous movie star and recipient of an Oscar who became Monaco's chief tourist attraction after she became Prince Rainier's wife, died just as tragically in a car crash. Beautiful Tina Livanos' incredible wealth, two marriages and a divorce must have caused her so much pain that she opted for suicide. Incredibly beautiful Elizabeth Taylor's star-studded celebrity life is riddled with ugly divorces, sudden deaths of her beloved friends, alcoholism and continuous physical pain from illnesses. Refreshingly beautiful and famous Lana Turner's numerous bad marriages and divorces were not enough—she had to go through the devastating ordeal of having the man she loved stabbed to death by her own daughter. Classically beautiful, wealthy and privileged (to a dizzying degree) Gloria Vanderbilt, Barbara Hutton, Barbara Paley and Marjorie

Merriweather Post all suffered betrayals by the men they loved and married. Rose Fitzgerald Kennedy's share of tragedy to offset the same set of gifts is stunning—she lost four children at their prime, two from plane crashes and two from assassination. Joan Bennett Kennedy, possessing these gifts to a slightly lesser degree, suffered the silent agony of a loveless marriage to a political celebrity, and the public stigma and private hell of alcoholism. Imelda Marcos paid dearly for her billions and celebrity status and such gifts as beauty and a beautiful singing voice—she went through the horrors of an assassination attempt, a coup d'etat, sudden downfall and banishment, ugly gossips and now court trials that may end in a long jail term for her. Princess Diana is presently paying for her stupendous gifts from nature via a turbulent marriage and the exhausting public life of the Princess of Wales. Anne Morrow Lindbergh, who added the dazzling achievement of being author and poet and beloved wife of America's dashing hero, Charles Lindbergh, to her already full chest of gifts, experienced a most grievous pain in return for all these—she lost her first child, Charles, Jr. to a kidnapper who accidentally killed the infant when he slipped from the ladder he used in abducting him. The body of the child was later dug out from a shallow grave after months of agonizing search. And what about Evita Peron? Her beauty, her position as Argentina's First Lady, her youth, her talents (some of which were questionable, according to her movie-biography), the fame and adulation she received which bordered on cult-worship—did she get a deadly prick from a spinning wheel needle for all these? She did. She died of cancer at age 32. The same deadly minus was what Nancy Leeds, monickered "American Princess," found at the bottom of her jar of fairy bounty. Cancer, too, ended her life of unrestrained opulence, glitter and royalty at age 45, vanquishing her physical beauty and her bubbling personality of wit and charm. Vivien Leigh, the dazzlingly beautiful British actress who won the plum role of Scarlet O'Hara after the two- year expensive and much-publicized talent search conducted by MGM, did not just have fame and wealth and talent. She also won Sir Laurence Olivier, the man she loved, from his beautiful wife, the actress Jill, whom he dumped in her favor in spite of the fact that she was carrying their first child. These cannot be forgiven by the negative forces. How did they bring her down to the level of ordinary mortals after she reached the heights of unrestrained splendor? By a most crippling, most humiliating, single minus—insanity. Thereafter, she lost everything Nature had given her. Sir Laurence Olivier divorced and abandoned her in her time of greatest need; then other losses followed—youth, beauty, fame, wealth, and then life itself. She died from tuberculosis without ever recovering from the ravages of schizophrenia.

This green goblin, envy, does not just wreak havoc in its capacity as an unseen demon. It takes the form of mortals, too, in the persons of relatives and friends. Snow White was "murdered" twice by her stepmother just because Snow White was more beautiful than she. Cinderella was punished with hard labor in her own house for her beauty by her ugly step-sister and step-mother. Psyche, who stood out in beauty, wealth and fortune from among her sisters, lost Cupid, her husband, through their envious machinations. Of course, these are just fairy tales and a myth from Greece. Since hard facts beat fiction, following are some facts that would put Psyche's case to shame:

Mary, Queen of Scots, had the lethal combination of Princess Aurora's gifts—beauty, charisma, royal pedigree, intelligence and popularity—specially with the opposite sex. Envy did not miss this conspicuous target. It took the form of her less endowed cousin, the homely Elizabeth I of England, who had her imprisoned for 19 years and finally had her killed off most gruesomely by beheading.

Marie Antoinette is an even better example. Her combined gifts exactly matched those of Mary, Queen of Scots, and became, therefore, irresistible to envy which took the form of her brother-in-law, Count D'Artois. He denounced her and her husband—his brother, Louis XVI— as enemies of the French Republic composed of starving and therefore insanely envious subjects. The guillotine chopped off her head and ended her life of glamor and luxury.

Another tragic example is Empress Alexandra Fedorovna, the wife of the last Tsar of Imperial Russia, Nicholas II. She was beautiful (a look-alike of Grace Kelly), brilliant, an accomplished pianist, blue-blooded (being the granddaughter of Queen Victoria of England), who presided over glittering balls in palaces consisting of 900 rooms all reeking of incomparable luxury—and who enjoyed the total love and devotion of her husband, the Tsar. Envy this time took the form of the Bolsheviks —the people they ruled who rose up in an unchecked revolution against imperialism and massacred her whole family after two years' imprisonment at Ekaterinburg. Their bullet-riddled and bayonetted bodies were further chopped into pieces, burned and thrown down a mine shaft by their pitiless executioners who were no other than their own bodyguards.

Cleopatra, history's Queen of the Nile, had been gifted with such beauty as to have caught the eyes and hearts of the two most powerful men of her time—Julius Caesar, emperor of the Roman empire, and Mark Antony, a celebrated general. This beauty was fatally combined with political brilliance, power and wealth, and led to her suicide at age 33 after defeat by her envious enemies.

A young maid from France who had these extraordinary gifts except wealth and pedigree was just as brutally murdered by envy in the form of the very people she had served. She was denounced as a witch and burned at the stake when her popularity reached adulation and overshadowed that of the most prominent people in her country, namely, King Charles VII, who owed his crown to her, and the French clergy, the power behind the throne. This was Joan of Arc.

Envy doesn't limit its curse to women. Men, too, have suffered and/or died from its virulence. There was David—who became the Bible's megastar when he killed Goliath. His youth, good looks, fine musicianship and his stupendous feat in defeating Goliath catapulted him to fame and adulation. When his fans began singing his praises, "Saul has slain his thousands, David his ten thousands," envy reared its ugly head and took the form of King Saul—the person who benefitted most from David's musicianship and military feat. Saul became obsessed with David's blood. He relentlessly pursued him to slay him, so that life suddenly became a long nightmare of flight for the young megastar until Saul's death put a merciful end to it. Even then, envy finished David off by mixing lust in his already overflowing cup. His scandalous affair with Bathsheba, wife of one of his generals, marred his greatness. And his son by her—Absalom—caused him such piercing grief when he openly defied his authority. Absalom formed his own army which fought against his father's and he openly used and abused David's harem. Oddly enough, when this repugnant offspring died an untimely death, David was inconsolable, prompting his advisers and the wise men of his time to shake their heads and rebuke him in public.

Jesus Christ's death was caused by envy, too, come to think of it. He possessed powers none of the "holy men" of His time could match. He was mobbed wherever he went, and was acclaimed "Son of God." This was too much for the green goblin, which immediately took the form of one of His own chosen friends—Judas Iscariot—and the Pharisees and the Sadducees, the holy men of the Jews. Together, they crucified the Greatest Man who ever lived on earth.

Johann Sebastian Bach, who had the gift of great musical genius, suffered for this from the hands of his own elder brother who locked up his music sheets to curtail Bach's genius from blossoming. Bach had to sneak up to the desk where the sheets were hidden and copied them by moonlight, every night. This eventually led to his partial blindness. When he was found out, he was ejected from his brother's house and he had to struggle against poverty for the rest of his life due to the handicap he acquired from his brother's envy.

Do you think Al Capone got lynched by the law? I am tempted to think that he got lynched by Mr. Green Goblin in the person of a police officer whose zeal in pinning him down was fueled more by envy than by love for justice. Of course, Al Capone was a crook who deserved what he got. But he wouldn't have met his end so soon if he had not flaunted his ill-gotten wealth so flagrantly and showed off his good looks, criminal brilliance and notoriety so flamboyantly. You see, this green imp does not just prey on good people. He garnishes his fare with wicked ones, too, for variety. The ones he leaves alone are the unendowed. They're too bland for his taste buds, like Wallis Simpson, the Duchess of Windsor, who became the greatest celebrity of the century when King Edward VIII of Britain relinquished his throne for her, and Queen Victoria and Queen Elizabeth I who had absolute power and pedigree, but, alas, had no physical beauty to complete the lethal dose necessary to whet his appetite. All three homely ladies were allowed by fate to be outlived by their wealth and titles. They all died from old age, after a good life punctuated by little sorrows, not big tragedies.

Then, of course, there's Charles Lindbergh, American hero. His tragedy has been discussed in the previous paragraphs.

Animals are not beyond this green goblin's line of vision, mind you. He also pounces on creatures that are gifted by nature with something of value. Else why are elephants, peacocks, ostriches, buffalo, reptiles, beavers, leopards, minks, sables and musks becoming alarmingly extinct? Because elephants have ivory tusks; peacocks and ostriches have fabulous feathers; buffalo and reptiles have hides for leather; beavers, leopards, minks and sables have expensive coats of fur; and musks have the ingredient for expensive perfume.

And why are dogs and cats cossetted and not murdered like their better-endowed fellow-creatures mentioned above? For the simple reason that they have nothing of commercial value for anyone to covet.

So, next time you are maligned or snubbed or "done in" by friends and relatives, or both, when you have done nothing against them, think! You must have done something they cannot equal. Or you must be carrying in your person a lethal dose of this green goblin's favorite diet—physical beauty, a spark of genius somewhere, pedigree, fame, privilege, love and adulation. With this green monster around, you're lucky not to have been murdered yet. Or not to have yet experienced tragedy experienced by the Auroras in the past, to offset your running away with just too much.

"Lightning always strikes the tallest building," observed Ovid two thousand years ago. He is right. Too much Spring does not fall in with Nature whose harmony is always kept in check by unseen forces. These forces are there so that we have the months equally apportioned among the seasons and Spring and Winter do not detract from each other's due. They are the "equalizers," the counterparts of "compensators." What is compensation? When you are conspicuously deficient in some necessary tool for survival, like eyesight, brains, health, a hidden force called "compensation" makes up things for you in the form of a stupendous talent or a stroke of luck. An idiot savant who could not lift a fork to feed himself could play piano concertos more brilliantly than any renowned pianist, just by listening to a recording of these but once. Helen Keller, triply handicapped (she was blind, deaf and dumb), emerged to become one of the greatest humanitarians the world has ever produced. Elizabeth Barrett Browning was handicapped by poor health and was terrorized by a tyrant of a father. She was compensated for these by a gift for poetry and by the love and devotion of her husband, Robert Browning. Their true-to-life love story remains unsurpassed by all the Romeos and Juliets who have ever lived on stage or off.

The hidden law of compensation does not manifest itself in people alone but also in geography. Africa's status as a Third World region is compensated for by its wealth in diamonds and game. Saudi Arabia's deserts yield oil which buys not only the water they don't have but also the luxuries the water-rich countries can't afford. Switzerland's dearth of natural resources is compensated for by its population of remarkably resourceful people. That's Nature's way.

Equalizers. Compensators. Together, they make this world go round to complete the mathematical equation that's behind the symphony of the universe. Does this make it easier for you (ye beautiful, powerful, and famous people) to accept envy as a necessary part of life? After all, envy is a vindictive tribute to your pluses. It's negative, but a tribute, nevertheless, and a help (a levelling force) to pull you back to earth well below the abode of invisible forces above, where dwell the demigods that make gifts of lightning bolts to those who dare come too near their threshold. Where angels fear to tread, mortals must approach with great trepidation.

24

On Marriage and Divorce

"A union of souls is often more easily
accomplished outside of marriage."
—Elizabeth Forsythe Hailey
Author, *A Woman of Independent Means*

AFTER READING WITH SPECIAL INTEREST the stand of Jose Jr. and Anita Meily against divorce and annulment in the 9 December 1984 issue of *Panorama*, I feel I must put down my reactions to it on paper.

It seems their religious zeal has made them somehow myopic, in the sense that they are more concerned with an institution (marriage) rather than with human beings. They are against divorce and annulment because these "allow a second marriage and will cheapen marriage." But they are not against the idea of couples separating and living in with their respective partners "if they wish to." In other words, they'd rather watch human beings cheapen themselves by living in adultery, than have the noble institution of marriage cheapened. Anyway, according to them, "God will judge them accordingly, with justice and mercy." They do not see the fact that the present (society's judgment) is just as important as the future (God's judgment). This is like saying, "Go ahead and get crippled today. Tomorrow, I'll buy you a wheelchair." In the Philippines, separated couples who swim out of the sea of a dead marriage into the solace of the shores of a new relationship are society's outcasts. In my opinion, adultery (which cheapens anyone who indulges in it and makes them outcasts) is the bigger evil than divorce or annulment which merely "cheapens" an institution like marriage, if it really does.

Is divorce or annulment really wrong? Let us consider an opinion of Joseph Murphy, a lay preacher:

God is not present in all marriages; perhaps there were ulterior motives in the union. If a man marries a woman for money, for

113

position, or to satisfy his ego, that marriage is false; and if a woman marries a man for security, wealth, position, a thrill, or to get even with someone else, such a marriage is not of God; for God, or the Truth, was not present. Such marriages are not real because they are not based on love. ("No love can be bound by oath or covenant to secure it against a higher love," says Ralph Waldo Emerson. Quotations mine.) Where there is a real, true, heavenly marriage—a union of hearts, minds and bodies—there can be no divorce. Neither do they seek divorce, for it is a spiritual union, it is a union of two hearts; they are united in love. ("Do you love me? means, do you see the same truth? If you do, we are happy with the same happiness: but presently one of us passes into the perception of new truth; we are divorced, and no tension in nature can hold us to each other," Emerson further elucidates. Quotations mine.)

Therefore, to say that annulment or divorce is "an insult to the Lord who created and designed marriage" is simply not logical, because He did not create all marriages. No marriage which God has put together can ever be put asunder by any man. As Taylor Caldwell put it in her novel *Bright Flows the River*, "No one can destroy a good sound marriage; it takes the combatants." The fact that some marriages have been put together by deceit (It does not much signify whom one marries as one is sure to find next morning that it is someone else," facetiously observed Samuel Rogers, in Liz Greene's book *Relating*) by either one of the parties, or both, makes them adulterous ("Ma, it wasn't adultery. They loved each other. You and Pa never loved each other, and so your living together was the real adultery, the spiritual one."—*Bright Flows the River*) and null and void from the beginning. ("I've always thought that a feeling which changes never existed in the first place," opines Ayn Rand in her mammoth tour de force, *Atlas Shrugged*.) Breaking this lie publicly by divorce or annulment is not an insult to God and society. On the contrary, it is heroic, just and necessary. ("Hell, son, a man who is faithful to his wife when he detests her is violating the great Law of Love, which rules the universe."—*Bright Flows the River*)

Furthermore, the break-up of most marriages here and in the West is not due to the presence of divorce, contrary to what the Meilys think. It is due to the advent of the Third Wave civilization in which we are caught, according to Alvin Toffler, celebrated social critic, in his bestseller, *The Third Wave*. Whereas the First Wave (Agricultural Society) had its "extended family" composed of grandparents, uncles, aunts, and cousins, aside from the main family, and the Second Wave (Industrial

Society) had its "nuclear family" composed of only the parents and their children—the present Third Wave (Superindustrial Society) has its family pared down to its most basic component: the individual. Thus, the disturbing rise of single parents and new arrangements that make up a strange lifestyle.

The onslaught of this Third Wave (a natural consequence of industrialism) calls for a sharp perception on our part to re-evaluate and re-structure our existing institutions and beliefs, according to the changes in our society. Change always brings with it the destruction of things familiar, therefore, confusion and suffering are inevitable. Yet, survival is definite for those of us who are willing to see clearly; for those of us who are willing to jettison all our cherished extra luggage, composed mainly of catechetical beliefs, so that, unfettered by the weight of these, we shall be able to swim to safety.

Let us then get rid of the weight of the following dangerous cargo:

—false premises, like "All marriages are created by God";
—wrong fears that divorce will encourage the break-up of marriages;
—challengeable statistics on teenage suicide attributed to divorced parents;
—baseless warnings that "adjustment is more difficult in a second union."

And, travelling light, our vision unbefogged by overzealousness, we shall be able to find true happiness in a marriage created by God. ("...and thou shalt be known only to thine own, and they shall console thee with tenderest love."—Ralph Waldo Emerson). Let us then move along the current of change, not against it. Only if we do so can we successfully ride this Third Wave and preserve the most sacred entity of all—our God-like selves.

25

Music—A Fifth Force in the Universe

(Closing remarks, Christmas Musicale,
Philippine Independent Church,
Lingayen, Pangasinan, 30 December 1987)

RT. REV. AND MRS. EDILBERTO BAUTISTA, our Emcee, Atty. Leonardo Jimenez, who delivered the very inspiring Opening Remarks, Faculty members of Harvent School, our guest pianists and performers, our young recitalists, ladies and gentlemen:

Thank you for coming and for providing us with an enthusiastic audience. (Note: The author played Nicanor Abelardo's First Nocturne.) Special thanks go to the parents of the participants in this afternoon's recital, for showing their wholehearted support not just for music in general but for artistry on the keyboard in particular.

There is something in the piano that other musical instruments don't have: its demands. Whereas one can play the guitar, the drums or the banduria after just a few lessons, one can become a pianist only after years and years of backbreaking work. Because unlike its sister string instruments which have only a few strings, the piano has a hundred strings attached to its ninety- two keys in its entire diapason.

Therefore, playing the piano is not just a skill or an art. It is championship. It demands years of sustained effort towards self-discipline and the joyful willingness to spend long hours of hard work practising and practising—which only a true champion can do. So that playing the piano is not an end in itself or done for art's sake. It is more than that. It is a process of expressing an achievement in self-realization—a celebration of one's being alive—of one's heroism.

I am proud to bring to your attention the fact that the guest pianists and organists who performed for you this afternoon had all been young beginners like the children presented in this recital. Mrs. Rosita Bautista who received her training from the country's best school of music—St. Scholastica's College, Manila—gave them the correct foundation on

116

which to build their artistry. They provided the rest—the joyful discipline and the long hours at the piano every day over many years. And, this afternoon, we heard them express that spirit of a champion deep within themselves.

A few years from now, new names will be added to the roster of our guest pianists—the latent champions whose young hands have already been given the spark by Mrs. Rosita Bautista and which spark will be fanned to burn ever brighter by the example of Yasmin Jimenez, Cesar Singson, Alfredo Gagaza and Mitzi Domingo. Had these young pianists lacked the spirit of championship necessary to subduing and enslaving a powerful force called music, we would not have been royally entertained this afternoon.

I would also like to thank the other musicians who made this afternoon's musicale unforgettable—the organists, guitarists and vocalists. Truly, music is alive and well because of them and we should be glad.

Music, my dear friends, has powers beyond any technology's reach. I like to call it the fifth force in the universe, the other four being the electro-magnetic force, the Weak force, the Strong force, and the gravitational force. Legends, historical and Biblical stories tell us of its fascinating powers.

Greek mythology recounts that a gifted musician named Orpheus almost succeeded in bringing back to life his beloved Eurydice through music. He played his lyre so magically that even the god and goddess of the dead fell under his spell. They were moved to tears by his lyre's description of his love for his wife and of his unbearable sadness at her leaving him all too suddenly that they allowed Eurydice to go back with him to the upperworld on only one condition: that he must not look back at her before they reached the upperworld. Cerberus, the three-headed watchdog of the underworld, was fast asleep (an unheard-of news in Hades), drugged by those sweet sounds, and did not pose any trouble when Orpheus and Eurydice made their hasty exit. But, alas, Orpheus looked back before they were out in the sunlight, and he lost his Eurydice forever.

Another story from Greek mythology tells us that music is indeed a force beyond our power to resist or control. It can reduce anyone to an unthinking idiot. Odysseus, that crafty hero of the Trojan War, almost did not make it home to his beloved Penelope. Midway on his voyage home to Ithaca was an island inhabited by sirens whose beautiful songs lured sailors to jump from their ships, never to be seen again. Knowing the danger they were about to face, Odysseus set his mind to work. He wanted to hear this song as much as he wanted to see his wife and son again. So he instructed all his men to put wax in their ears for their safety, and to lash him fast to the mast with stout ropes, because he was the only one without wax in his ears. He heard the magic song. Odysseus, a man famed for his presence of mind, suddenly became a suicidal fool. He frantically tried to set himself free and jump overboard and go to the island of the sirens. Such was the power of that music. The stout ropes and the brawn of his temporarily deaf sailors, however, saved him from sure death.

A legend from modern times makes a startling statement that the power of music has a practical value that cannot be duplicated by any technology based even on the advanced study of chemistry. The legend says that the prosperous but filthy city called Hamelin was infested with rats. The rats destroyed everything—their best furniture, their velvet clothes, their lace and silk curtains; they ransacked their storerooms of flour and cheese, and even bit the babies to death. The citizens used everything to eradicate this great problem: the most vicious rat poisons, the most complicated rat traps, and even the most barbaric way of clubbing them to death. None of these worked. But the hapless city was finally rid of its pests, so the legend goes, through music. A Piper played a tune on his pipe and all the rats joyfully, blindly followed him down to the river where they all drowned. This story is known as "The Pied Piper of Hamelin."

Another legend from China tells of a mortally sick emperor, pronounced to live only a few months longer by the royal physicians, who miraculously got well and lived on for many years after his gloomy sentence, all because a nightingale decided to sing on the bough of a tree across his window every morning and evening. This story is in every child's collection of fairy tales and legends, entitled "The Nightingale."

History has its contribution, too. According to historical records from India, dating back to the 16th century, Akbar the Great had a gifted musician named Mujan Tan Sen who could envelop the palace precincts in total darkness at high noon by singing a raga. He could also quench fire just by singing a particular song. I believe if we unlock the files where his secret song is buried, we won't need the services of the fire department!

Finally, the Bible clinches this truth about the power of music in its account of how David, the slayer of Goliath, brought surcease to King Saul who was suffering from a mental illness (called manic depression by modern psychiatry), by playing on the lyre. David's music unfailingly brought him out of his dark, dangerous moods, the Bible says.

So music does not just soothe or entertain. It drugs one out of his right or wrong senses; it is a pesticide; it is a sleeping potion; it is a fire extinguisher; it confuses the hours so that midnight can be bidden by it to come at high noon; it can deliver one from insanity and even from death's door. And—who knows?—it may well be the force that will lead us to immortality.

These fascinating effects of music can be better understood if we realize that the universe runs on rhythm—that planets and stars, and the galaxies, in their movement, create music. "There is music in the spheres," says Guy L. Playfair, the author of *Cycles of Heaven*. Rhythm is the basic component of music and of every sound, heard or unheard, in the universe. Music is sound. It is a divine word. It has potent effect on us, if we consider the fact that we are an expression of the Creative Word, so says a Yogi, by the name of Paramahansa Yogananda. In the Bible, John the Evangelist traces our beginning to sound—

> In the beginning was the Word, and the
> Word was with God, and the Word was God.

Sound is vibrating energy or power. And vibrating energy that is in complete harmony with God's word is music.

Blessed are we then to have music with us in the course of our journey through this life.

May we be all around again to provide another proud audience for our new pianists and musicians next year. Until then, Merry Christmas and a Happy New Year!

26

Happiness, Not just Success

(Chosen by the Women's Journal *as one of the special gifts
to its readers, on the occasion of the 17th anniversary issue,
7 April 1990.)*

I HAVE, in my possession right now, about a thousand index cards filled with tips on how to succeed. I have collected them through the years, not just for my personal consumption, but for my children's and my pupils'. I had intended to write an article to help them become successes in life. But now, after having met and interacted with some successful people, I decided to teach them instead to be happy. For I have come to realize, after distilling my observations on life these past 40 years, together with the wisdom of the writers whose books I am fortunate to have read, that a happy person is a hundred times better than a successful person. The truly happy person is very rare in a world filled with successful people, because successful people are not necessarily always happy. Success, here, means simply getting what one wants in life.

Happiness is rare because it cannot be found anywhere except within oneself. (And very few ever care to explore that special, unknown region.) It cannot be found in another person through romantic love. How many have killed themselves and destroyed others because of love? "Happiness and unhappiness have nothing to do with love," avers Hugh Walpole, author of *Vanessa.* "Love caused more suffering than it was worth—perhaps," bemoans Taylor Caldwell in her novel, *Bright Flows the River.* "Romance!" scoffs Belva Plain in her novel, *Evergreen,* "Emotional peaks, high moments. How long do they last? They're unreal." Yes, the highs they do give are unreal, but the pain they also give is very real. You only break your heart when you fall in love. All lovers will agree with me on this.

It cannot be found in marriage. "The wisest men in the world often seemed plagued by marital troubles," observed Ernest Gann in his novel

120

Masada. James Clavell thinks so, too. In *Noble House* he concedes that marriage is "exhausting even to a good man." Divorce statistics confirm this. Nor can happiness be found in adultery, because "adultery can be as boring as marriage," shares Helen Gurley Brown, who mentions in her book, *Having It All,* that she had been "kept" by a married man for sometime. In fact, adultery and trouble are synonymous so that novelists lace their plots with love triangles for the imperative flavor of trouble to make their books sell.

It can't be found in voluntary singlehood, within the convent or in caves, either. Danielle Steele, that dynamo of a novelist, says in *Changes,* one of her two dozen novels, "It isn't always easy being alone . . . neither is being together." How many ex-nuns and ex-priests have you met? I have met several. And I have read of rebel priests up in the mountains who surely cannot be called happy. Rebels are angry people. And angry people are incapable of happiness.

Happiness cannot be found in celebrity-status, nor in fame and power which are the world's final yardsticks of success. These are all temporary, like flashes in a pan, if taken in the context of eternity. Oftentimes, these are accidental, not hard-earned and, therefore, the satisfaction they give is shallow. Movie stars and royalties are some of the unhappiest people in the world. Their private disasters are the grist of gossip mills around the world, and their sudden deaths from suicide and drunken driving regularly shock ordinary people like you and me. Ferdinand Marcos' power led to his whole family's exile and to three years of living death. When he finally died, he was denied the peace and the proper resting place in his native country that ordinary mortals are given. The sudden fame of Charles Lindbergh led to a most grievous pain—an envious person kidnapped and accidentally killed his infant son. Margaret Mitchell, author of *Gone with the Wind,* could not adjust to a normal life after fame wrecked her peace and domesticity, according to her biography, *Road to Tara,* by Anne Edwards.

Happiness cannot be found in money. "Great wealth," says novelist Belva Plain, in her novel *Evergreen,* is a "frightful handicap" which "insulates you from living." "Beyond a decent minimum level, money fails to bring us what we think it will," observes Sydney J. Harris in an old *Reader's Digest* article. With these in mind, we should not wonder, therefore, at the celebrated unhappiness of heiresses Christina Onassis, Barbara Hutton, Gloria Vanderbilt and Anne Marie Rasmussen ex-Rockefeller, the housemaid who married for money and lost it and her husband a few years later, through divorce. "Did you get your money by fraud?" asks Ayn Rand in *Atlas Shrugged.* "By pandering to men's vices or men's stupidity?" she specifies. "By catering to fools, in the hope of getting more than your ability deserves? By lowering your standards? By doing work you despise for purchasers you scorn? If so, then your money will not give you a moment's or a penny's worth of joy. Then all the things you buy will become, not a tribute to you, but a reproach; not an achievement, but a reminder of shame," she further elucidates. "Money is the product of virtue, but it will not give you virtue and it will not redeem your vices," she warns. Pilar, Corazon and Maria (not their real names), women I know who got "rich" in the very manner described by Ayn Rand above, admit to being unhappy during their unguarded moments. "What destroyed me and led me to where I am now was the first man I had loved . . ." Corazon once soliloquized in my presence. She got her money and position (by themselves, unremarkable) unvirtuously, to make up for her dismal family background and for having been jilted before, and she knows it and she's not happy.

The temporary "highs" we get from romantic love, money, power, fame, and privilege can never substitute for the permanence and depth of the real happiness we get from a full recognition of our worth as a human being. And where do we get our worth as a human being? All writers agree there's one good source—through our work. The work we like to do (not the job we are forced to do) and choose to do to express and make use of our intellectual ability inevitably makes us like our self, and self-approval makes us happy. This kind of work that we shall call PLAY, because of its very definition, enables us to taste this rare delicacy called happiness, for we use our *own* powers and thus become powerful and confident. Our work removes the immoral shortcut of using others and allowing others to use us, from our list of options to "get ahead." Stated differently, it removes the temptation of degrading methods weaker individuals resort to. Work is dignity—the only dignity. Nothing is as much fun as achieving," exalts Helen Gurley Brown in her discovery, after she became the author of the bestseller, *Sex and the Single Girl,* and thence editor of *Cosmopolitan* magazine, American career women's Bible. This observation is re-echoed by Thomas Edison's father who had been quoted as saying, "Accomplishing something provides the only real satisfaction in life." Jules Renard says the same thing in different words: "I know only one truth—work alone creates happiness. I am sure only of that one thing . . ." "If you always put your heart into everything you do," advises actor Alan Alda, in his address to the graduating class of which his daughter was a member, "you really can't lose. Whether you wind up making a lot of money or not, you will have had a wonderful time, and no one will ever be able to take that away from you." Of course, this can only happen if you happen to be expressing your own unique talents constructively. The work you'll be doing will be something you really love. It is play.

Aside from constructive, purposeful play, there is another source of happiness, and it is learning. Learning outside the confines of school. "You can live longest and best and most rewardingly by attaining and preserving the happiness of learning. Many who avoid learning, or abandon it, find that life is drained dry," noted Gilbert Highet in his article, "The Immortal Profession."

Play (the work we love to do in expressing our talents) and learning can be pursued only through solitude. The truly happy person, then, is the one who loves to immerse himself/herself in the bliss of solitude —for that is where all achievements and wisdom spring from. In solitude, alone-ness becomes a sacred state, in contrast with the pain of loneliness which weak, unproductive persons feel, even in the company of others.

There is integrity in play and learning, and "regardless of fame, money, power or any of the conventional yardsticks—if you seek and find integrity, you ARE a success," says Arthur Gordon. Integrity comes from the word integral, meaning, WHOLE. You are whole if you do not lessen or cheapen yourself for money and power. Because once you do, no money or power on earth can make you happy. Learn and play. They insulate you against selling yourself short. They integrate your talents and mind and soul together, making you a whole person. And only a whole person can be truly happy.

Why is it so important to be happy? Well, it is a medical fact that happy people are healthy people. In his book *Return of the Rishi*, Dr. Deepak Chopra points out that "Modern medical studies repeatedly show that being happy is excellent protection against illness. The positive emotions apparently set up a basic biochemistry in the nervous system that directly enhances the body's ability to ward off sickness and combat it when it appears." Sydney J. Harris seconds this notion by saying, "A man whose work is emotionally satisfying can cope with a great deal of tension in other areas of his life. If he feels that he is making a contribution, if he feels that the intangible returns from his work compensate for the long hours and the lesser pay, he has a secret source of strength to sustain him." True. Of what use is money, power and fame if, like Ferdinand Marcos, you can't enjoy them because you're hooked to tubes in a hospital bed? Work (the kind we have re-named PLAY) rewards the worker (player) with sound sleep, a wholesome digestion and powers that are kept at their best. "The only things you regret (and feel unhappy about) are what you didn't do," according to Helen

Gurley Brown. People who love to work live to be above 90. There's Grandma Moses, Pablo Casals, Robert Frost, Rubinstein, Paderewski, Sir Winston Churchill, Justice Oliver Wendell Holmes—all masters of their particular craft. They worked joyfully and hard, up to their last breath. In other words, they spent their whole life at play. Some great players like them get well-rewarded with money. Some do not. Yet they are all rewarded fully through their enjoyment of the process of attainment which far outweighs the financial rewards.

Are we now ready to define what happiness is? Let's make the master authors do it for us. From Ayn Rand's *Atlas Shrugged*, we have a definite definition of happiness:

> Happiness is not to be achieved at the command of emotional whims. Happiness is not the satisfaction of whatever irrational wishes you might blindly attempt to indulge. Happiness is a state of non-contradictory joy—a joy without penalty or guilt, a joy that does not clash with any of your values and does not work for your own destruction, not the joy of escaping from your mind, but of using your mind's fullest power, not the joy of faking reality, but of achieving values that are real, not the joy of a drunkard, but of a producer. Happiness is possible only to a rational man, the man who desires nothing but rational actions.
>
> Just as I support my life, neither by robbery nor alms, but by my own effort, so I do not seek to derive my happiness from the injury or the favor of others, but earn it by my own achievement.

Let us clinch this beautiful topic on happiness with another definition, given by the world's most respected psychologist, Wilson Mc-Dougall, as quoted by June Callwood in her article, "The One Sure Way to Happiness":

> Happiness is an achievement, brought about by inner productiveness.
>
> Hollow people, lacking any conviction of their worth and self-respect, have nothing to give—a profoundly unhappy state.
>
> The richer, the more highly developed, the more completely unified or integrated is the personality, the more capable it is of sustained happiness, in spite of intercurrent pains of all sorts.

To do my job as a parent and as an educator well, I have chosen to deal with happiness rather than with success, because there is more challenge in producing happiness than mere success. It is easier to succeed than to be happy. There are shortcuts to success. None to happiness. The main ingredient of success—money—is easier to get (you can marry it, win it, stumble upon it, inherit it, grab it, or beg for it) than the main ingredient of happiness which is self-respect. Self-respect can only be earned, never inherited, stumbled upon, married, grabbed, or solicited. It's easy to be rich. It's so hard to be a real person. It takes book knowledge to succeed. It takes self-knowledge to be happy.

To be happy. "That," declares Ayn Rand, "is your only moral duty. Look at the earth as a place of enjoyment, and always keep in mind that the work of achieving one's happiness is the purpose, the sanction and the meaning of life."

Be truly happy, first, then. Know yourself, so you can play and learn all day long. Then, if you care about them, those pillars of success—fame and fortune—will follow at your happy, busy heels, like excited puppies about to take a walk with their beloved master. For happy people are always successful, and not the other way around.

I wish my readers happiness, not just success!

27

Double Take!

(My own "unholy" pronouncements)

Formal Education

THE GREATEST STEP towards success is self-knowledge—knowing one's purpose based on the knowledge of one's abilities and limitations. On this count alone, graded schools are guilty of having prevented their graduates from taking this crucial step towards success because they "lost" their self-knowledge in the crowd of the class, having been systematically re-designed to function uniformly as members of the class/the student body—a soul-less, brainless entity, and not as individuals. Their individuality—their soul and unique personality and consciousness—had been obliterated and sacrificed for a standard mentality and a standard behavior that cannot be used for coping with real situations outside that standard.

* * *

How can democratic countries like the U.S.A., the Philippines, Australia, and some European countries support the graded system of education whose very concept is anti-democratic? The whole system is a conspiracy against the individual. It robs the individual of choice because of its required curriculum and attendance. It penalizes the thinkers and creators. It does not respect individual differences but worships the uniformity of collectivism because of the "standard" it imposes. Its whole philosophy is communistic—it focuses on the class, the student body, the school, never on the individual.

* * *

Who is responsible for making Filipinos, including the so-called intelligent ones, limit their dreams and potentials to "finishing my

126

studies"? Do they really want to put an end to their education and switch on the inevitable process of decay? Education has no end. It can never be finished. Only death can give education its rightful conclusion.

* * *

Education comes from the Latin word "educo" which means "to lead out"—of darkness and ignorance, of bondage and suffering. But, if schools do lead anyone out, it is from enlightenment, from freedom. Many schooled people are ignorant because either they cannot read or because they have developed an aversion to books and a deep resentment towards learning due to the violent process they underwent in the classroom. Many are mental slaves—to stupid traditions and practices, beliefs, and rules and regulations formulated by feeble-minded authorities for their kind. Hence, education authorities are anti-intellectual dictators. The menace they visit on the youth is real and crippling, for life.

* * *

The non-graded school is the only institution that attempts to tackle what the graded schools refuse to do, and cannot do—educate the individual child. In the face of economic depression where all adult family members have to go out and work, nobody is left to teach the school children the basics. This is why, what wasn't too obvious before has become obvious now: the graded school fails to teach the basics. How can it? Basic skills can only be taught on a one-to-one basis, not on a one-to-fifty basis. To camouflage its failure, the graded school uses homework and teaches unnecessary information to the detriment of the pupil and the parents. This failure wasn't so obvious in the past because there was always someone in the home to teach the basics. Now that there aren't any, this incompetence sticks out.

* * *

The invisible is more powerful than the visible. No wonder self-education, which takes place in an invisible university called Life, under invisible teachers called Nature and Experience, is what tycoons and great men have in common. Mediocres and failures, on the other hand, have, for their Alma Mater, very visible universities made of brick buildings and green campuses and visible multi-degreed teachers called professors and Doctors. Those in between, the almost great, had both the visible and the invisible kinds of education.

* * *

Mass education. Compulsory education. Do our authorities and intelligent citizens realize these are all a big joke? No soul-less entity can ever get educated. Education can only be pursued by an individual who has the soul, the unique mind and disposition to desire and absorb and make use of it. It can never be compelled. For this reason, formal education (graded schools and universities) ought to be re-spelled as E-JOKE-ATION, education authories and "graded-school" teachers, E-JOKE-CATORS.

* * *

We require high school kids to study Economics in spite of the dismal fact that we owe our poverty to our economists (those technocrats who have MA's and PhD's in Economics from Harvard, Stanford, Wharton, etc.) who have deliberately or undeliberately hocus-pocused our economy.

* * *

We support medical schools and hospitals and pharmaceutical companies and revere doctors when, in fact, five million deaths in the U.S.A. alone between 1981 to 1987 had been directly caused by medical treatment, i.e., wrong diagnosis, overdose, rusty and dirty hospital equipment, hospital contagion, unnecessary operations. This is three times more than the casualties of World War II and the Vietnam War put together, says Dr. Deepak Chopra (prominent Indian endocrinologist from Boston and author of *Quantum Healing, Creating Health* and *Return of the Rishi*) who disclosed this fact to an awe-struck audience at the Hong Kong International Convention Center, composed of doctors and prominent social leaders from all over Asia last 28 July 1989.

* * *

Values

The reason why we suffer in life is due to the fact that we value the wrong things:

—We value information instead of skills for further learning and the development of higher mental processes. Look at the required curriculum. Who's complaining about it? Only yours truly.

—We value certification instead of education. If we got rid of degrees and diplomas, no one will want to go to school.

—We value science scholars, instead of scientists.

—We value a dialect, instead of a language.

—We value credentials instead of true ability.

—We value awards instead of achievements.

—We engender competition among pupils instead of cooperation.

—We cling to trusted myths instead of facts and happily let them guide us to perdition.

—We polish and glamorize wrong systems instead of demolishing them.

—We love to "finish" our studies instead of devoting our whole life to learning some more.

—We love well-rounded freaks like valedictorians and summa cum laudes instead of normal, lopsided people whose excellence in only one thing accounts for our comforts in life.

—We love authorities who blindfold us through life and hate the thinkers and innovators who are their unmaskers and our blind-fold removers.

—We love charades like graded schools and hate the reality that learning takes place outside of these.

—We love excuses like "It's impossible!" "It's the system and we can't change it!" "It's the rule. I'm only implementing it." "It's the best I can do." "I tried, but . . ." "It has been practised for 300 years, so it must be correct."

—We love public approval, above our own.

—We spend a great deal of money and time earning MA's and PhD's instead of polishing our unique talents.

—We allow schools and universities to kill off our originality and outlook.

—We allow schools to reward obedience, studiousness, standard mentality, and uniformity when, in fact, life rewards none of these, but the opposite: creativity, originality, repudiation of the old and familiar, search for the new and different, and independence—traits killed off by these formal institutions.

—We entrust our children's education and well-being to credentialled educators who give us a regular supply of illiterates and unemployable graduates each year.

—We value information, more than imagination.

—We value acceptance of facts, instead of challenging those facts.

—We value marriage, including bad marriages. Look at all those intelligent girls who marry beneath them, just so they can get a taste of this over-rated adventure/arrangement called marriage. Look at all those unhappily married people, who feel trapped and can't and won't get out. We must value only a good marriage, and must get out of a bad one. It is our moral duty to be happy and not allow anyone, much less an institution like marriage, to rob us of our peace and happiness.

—We value old, rusty beliefs, instead of new and different insights.

—We value wealth, instead of prosperity.

—We value success, instead of happiness.

—We value a religious believer, instead of a thinker.

—We value easy money more than earned money—the appearance of achievement instead of true achievement. Thus, many of us esort to the glamorous prostitution of marrying wealth, or becoming mistresses of the wealthy. Or we con and steal behind the pseudo-glamor of the organized crime of politics, or behind the profitable rackets of organized religion, patriotism, social work, formal education, medical practice.

—We love to suffer. Period. Else, why do we tolerate the status quo?

Marriage

Love is valuing. We fall in love with a person who reflects that which we value most. Our values do not remain the same. They change as we grow. This is why people fall in love not just once, but many times in their lifetime, unless they value the permanent bliss only solitude can bring. The young value physical beauty and the evidence of good family background. So their first love is the most beautiful girl or the most handsome boy from a good family. As they mature, their values change to something more abstract. They value achievement and competence. So they fall in love with achievers, whether these achievers are beautiful or not. As they get even more mature, this value changes again into something more subtle than achievement—communication beyond the intellectual level. So they fall in love with someone they can communicate with, who sees truth as they see it. In old age, all values change to just one—companionship. They will love anyone who will provide them company in their old age. Some old people experience a recycling of values. In their old age, they find themselves valuing physical beauty once again. So they pursue partners young enough to be their daughters/sons or grandchildren. Unless a husband and wife's values grow parallel with each other, or unless their values remain steady through the years, from their wedding day to the day they die, adultery becomes a reality. Divorce becomes a necessity to wash off the social stigma of adultery with the morality of a second or third marriage. This change of values is part of growth. As we grow, we change. If we unfortunately outgrow our spouse, no force in the universe can bind us together. We are divorced in the true sense of the word, officially or not, ostensibly or not.

* * *

Lucky is the spouse whose partner changes according to the change in his/her values, or who does not change when the partner does not. She or he is young and attractive when the partner values physical beauty. He/she has achievements to show when the partner values achievement. He/she is so well-read and open-minded as to be able to commune on all levels of consciousness when the partner has grown intellectually and spiritually and cosmically. He/she provides good company in old age and beats the young in over-all attractiveness of his/her whole personality and outlook.

* * *

Religion

If Jesus Christ came back to life now and sees that what He had stood for and worked for had degenerated into mere sectarianism, He would be deeply pained. He would feel ashamed of the bitter fact that instead of redeeming mankind from suffering, He had, instead, plunged them into more suffering (due to the twisting and scissoring off of His message by the Vatican, which His followers joyfully endorse in anticipation of the invisible carrots of a heaven after this life).

* * *

How can intelligent people entrust their life and happiness to religious leaders—seeking their advice, following their decrees about such vital issues as birth control and divorce—when these people don't even know them as well as they know themselves? How can these religious leaders speak on marriage and the home when most of them are not married and have no homes but communes called convents? How can they make stands on divorce and birth control when they are not personally affected by these issues and, therefore, cannot see the deeper ramifications of these issues? How can anybody ever willfully abdicate his God-given talent to discover reality and deliberately entrust his happiness to priests and nuns who can be more blind and ignorant than he? How can anyone who is not a fool put others above himself and allow them to live his life for him?

* * *

Money

Give money to a weak man and he'll corrupt himself and his. Give money to a strong man and he becomes a philanthropist. Or do it the other way around. Deprive them of money. The weak will promptly steal or sell his soul or becomes a parasite. The strong man will work and become a great inventor or achiever, enriching the world with his achievements as he enriches himself. You want to find out your true friend? Use money. Your true friend can never be bought. Your false friend will sell you eagerly for one cent and add his own soul into the bargain.

* * *

Wealth and prosperity are not the same. Wealth means possession of concrete things—millions in the bank, mansions in all the beautiful places, a dozen cars, yachts and private planes.

Prosperity is more than an economic condition. It is possession of an abstract value, a state of mind—of contentment with what one has, of the ability to control one's life and do the work one wants.

Wealth is poverty if it cannot insulate its possessor from misery; if it robs him of the time to enjoy his mansions and his family; if it prevents him from dealing with an aggravating person in the manner that person deserves for fear of losing his money; if it robs him of the choice to divorce the wife he has unfortunately outgrown and be with the woman he truly loves for fear of public sanction which will result in the loss of his position and income. His wealth, in this case, is indeed a burden. If a wealthy man has to lower his standards to suit his customers' unrefined taste, his wealth is a curse, not a blessing.

Prosperity is that condition that allows someone to do what he feels is right and enjoy every moment of it. Prosperity is the freedom one experiences in not doing things that go against the grain of one's upbringing. This condition makes him feel rich and fortunate.

Therefore, a wealthy man may feel deprived in spite of his earthly treasures, and a prosperous man may feel blessed and rich in spite of his lack of these.

28

Yours Truly

(A Candid Self-Portrait)

I am:

—a space traveller like everyone else in this round spaceship called planet Earth;

—an Aquarian, thus my unconventionality and unpredictability;

—a single parent to three growing children: Hilton, Yul and Farrah;

—an educator (Founder/Director of HARVENT SCHOOL, a non-traditional school for boys and girls);

—an author (*School Mythtakes,* copyright 1987; *Double Take!* copyright, 1990; and Fly with Me!);

—the editor/publisher, *The Magic Pencil,* an annual magazine for adults by children under 12;

—a Sidha, on my way to mastering more laws of nature;

—a TM teacher, lady governor of the Age of Enlightenment Foundation, (a world organization for World Health and World Peace);

—a pianist by avocation;

—a dabbler in charcoal painting;

—an amateur palmist;

—a happy individualist, lover of achievements and achievers;

—a risk-taker—I got married, remember? And I wrote and published my perilous thoughts;

—a dedicated non-conformist (an iconoclast, says my publisher);

—a bookworm, feeding on lofty thoughts;

—an excellent conspirator in mischiefs;

—naive about the dark side of human nature; and

—an impertinent human being to close-minded fools.

I am not:

—a joiner. The Age of Enlightenment Foundation is the only

organization I have ever seriously joined and stayed in the
longest;
—a blind follower;
—a politician (official or non-official) nor an admirer of one;
—a good nurse—convalescents turn comatose under my care;
—capricious; simple things please me most: fresh air, loose cotton
dusters, Gandharva music, something to read, big shady trees,
real flowers, green mangoes, *buko, butong pakwan*, dragon flies,
frogs' chorus;
—the coy and sweet type;
—easy to win over again after my respect and trust are lost.

I am afraid of:
—all religions and isms, especially communism and patriotism.
They spell suffering and death in holocaust proportions;
—the Philippines becoming a second Vietnam;
—man-made laws (marriage and divorce laws, labor laws, agrarian
reform laws). They are anti-life;
—wrong information. They're open manholes in my path;
—ignorance, stupidity and close-mindedness. They, not crime, are
the real threats to life;
—making the same mistake twice. I'd lose a big chunk of my self-
respect;
—deadlines. They give me ulcers;
—appearances. They're live coals coated with ashes;
—people who are neutral. They're neither right nor wrong. They're
evil;
—close friends. God himself was almost overthrown from his
heavenly throne by his favorite angel closest to him—Lucifer;
Samson owed his death to his friend, Delilah; Holofernes' to his
favorite wife, Esther; Jesus Christ's to one of his chosen—Judas;
Julius Caesar's to his favorite ward, Brutus; Nero's to his valet;
Mary, Queen of Scots', to her close relative, Elizabeth I;
Napoleon Bonaparte's to his aide who lived with him in exile;
Tsar Nicholas and his entire family's to their bodyguards; Pope
John Paul I's to the select coterie around him in the Vatican; *ad
infinitum, ad nauseam;*
—over-sensitive people. They give me negative vibrations I don't
deserve;
—being misunderstood. I lose a lot of goodwill and values;
—bargain sales. I end up with too many things I don't need;

—the sight of blood, snakes (real and illustrated), soldiers and
   policemen and their guns;
—a telephone's ring at midnight or early morning. Bad news!
—carrying cash with me;
—white hair. The six I have upset me;
—champagne and aspirin. They give me hives;
—the sun. It makes me smell like a lathered horse;
—walking under coconut trees. A heavy nut almost fell on me when
   I was little;
—dogs. They're too physical for comfort;
—driving my econovan—when the engine starts purring, my knees
   also start shaking;
—my imagination, sometimes. Uncontrolled, it can make me sick.
   An itch gives me the spectre of leprosy; a bruise, leukemia; a
   migraine, brain cancer; a lapse in memory, insanity;
—being second best in what I do;
—loans I cannot pay;
—malicious rumors. They can undercut a good business;
—figures and equations. They give me goose pimples, chills and
   migraine;
—old rusty beliefs. They give me lockjaw.

I am not afraid of:
   —the truth. It may hurt but it will never mislead;
   —hard work, as long as it's in my line of interest;
   —strange, dangerous ideas. They're the torch to a better lifestyle;
   —writing down and publishing my own share of strange,
      dangerous ideas, for exactly the same reason;
   —changes and breakups. They're always for the better;
   —losses and reversals. To me, they always precede a windfall in
      some other area in my life;
   —opinions of people who have not yet earned my respect and ad-
      miration or who have lost my respect and admiration.
   —confrontations. In a discussion, the truth always comes out;
   —calories. They make me look better.

I have:
   —an excellent education, 95% of which came from experience
      (personal and vicarious), leisurely reading and interaction with
      the right people, 5% from the expensive schools I attended

—Maryknoll College and the University of the Philippines,
   Quezon City;
—a vision for the individual's education which is not co-extensive
   with the education authorities' vision for the masses;
—my own kind of hotline to the Absolute;
—a natural turn for the Arts and Letters;
—done the smart and the foolish;
—experienced triumph and defeat (I am an utter failure in my attempts to make over some people), losses and gains, betrayal
   and loyalty, windfalls and reversals, and because of a new technology called TM, I experience a permanent sense of bliss;
—happy memories of childhood (those comic books in English
   which taught me English most effectively; Sister Mary Michael's
   stories; bicycle rides; the big brown one-centavo coin that could
   buy 2 *biscochos*, 2 candies, 1 lady's ring, 1 tiny plastic toy; paper
   centavos—5c, 10c, 20c ,and 50c; our maids who stayed for years
   and years, our drivers, too; the sound of horses' rhythmic clip-
   clops instead of the infuriating whir of these present-day
   motorized tricycles; our *bahay-kubo* and its kitchen and *batalan*
   where we cooked real food and washed real clothes with real
   soap all day long; our Java guava tree (the only tree I could
   climb); the sound of Hanon, Czerny and John Thompson on the
   piano; the sound of Papa's daily dose of Dvorak, Tchai-kowsky,
   Beethoven, Chopin, Callas; bathing in the rain with our
   geese; our family dogs, Mickey and Tiger, who knew how
   to keep quiet and to keep away from me; Papa's Spanish-speak-
   ing friends and relatives who dropped by regularly; Tia Cedes'
   war stories; Mama's noontime fantasy stories; the truckload of
   mangoes from the farms every summer (now we have to buy!);
   the love and respect of our tenants which have now turned
   to insolence; our sweet, sweet *suha* which endeared me to all my
   friends; *sungka* games with Tia Yayao; sharing secrets with Atche
   Patty (sniff! sniff!);
—a diary recording my first four years, written by my doting
   parents;
—my own private library and about 25,000 indexed notes from my
   readings;
—a collection of miniatures;
—10,000 photographs;
—seven baskets of make-up and cosmetics;
—two myopic eyes that work against my PR;

—a third eye, according to mystics;

—a fourth eye, for beauty;

—good taste that doesn't come from my tongue;

—two slim legs which can nevertheless support my ideals of independence;

—a cleft chin;

—a brown thumb. The greens I plant turn brown;

—a sour, not sweet, tooth. I prefer green mangoes to ice cream;

—very little patience. Slow-moving events and people drive me nuts;

—ominous silences that are more eloquent than words;

—a few major regrets all connected with my lack of patience and unbelievable naivete;

—lost about 2,000 ballpens; 1,000 umbrellas and 500 books (through lending) in my lifetime;

—travelled abroad;

—survived the praises of big people and the envy and betrayal of the small.

I love:

—solitude and what I accomplish because of it;

—rainy days and their particular music;

—my rocking chair where I mastermind my life and do my writing;

—letters and packages;

—my Macintosh SE and Imagewriter II—they're my most talented companions in life;

—romance and the fleeting magic it brings;

—the little money and recognition my talents have earned for me;

—legends. They're metaphysically true;

—my kids' awe at being alive;

—TM! doing it and its beautiful results;

—magic and magicians;

—fortune-tellers and astrologers;

—baby pictures of people I know;

—sunrise (the few I have seen) and sunset. They're so promising;

—men who love their work—happy men!

—shiny beetles;

—excellence;

—my independence and my retrieved freedom;

—Joe Salazar's talent in making us chic;

—good books. In between their covers are the lively minds of great

thinkers who provide me with the scaffolding on which I build
my own cathedral of thoughts;
—the pronouncements of fallible persons like Albert
Einstein, Ralph Waldo Emerson, George Bernard Shaw, and
Maharishi Mahesh Yogi, not necessarily in that order. They make
more sense than those of the "infallibles."
—short-cuts—the moral ones.

I dislike:
—religious organizations. I'd feel like a crab trapped in a punch
bowl in one;
—Manila traffic—makes me wish for an anti-gravity belt;
—animals in the house. They make me nervous;
—stupid traditions;
—lemons (products and people); a ballpen that doesn't write; a door
that doesn't close; an umbrella that doesn't open; a lighter that
doesn't light; incompetent employees; irresponsible spouses.
These should be given away to people only during April Fools'
Day, gift-wrapped and be-ribboned!
—soliciting funds;
—asking favors;
—lending my things;
—borrowing things;
—copycats;
—pseudo-intellectuals;
—Christ's stand on divorce;
—wigs, toupees, false eyelashes and false fingernails—they are tom-
foolery carried too far;
—loose change. They're so heavy and worthless, like old beliefs and
false friends;
—the funny pronouncements of "infallible" persons;
—detours.

I can:
—change misfortune into a blessing;
—do anything I set my mind on;
—get whatever I want desperately most of the time;
—fight for my principles as ruthlessly as Genghis Khan;
—take risks and win;
—go out of my way to help a friend in trouble;

_change my mind regarding minor issues at a confusing rate but always with the best results in mind;
—keep secrets that I'm told to keep;
—drive a good bargain;
—be fooled, but not for long and woe to the fooler for his/her presumption;
—persuade intelligent people, never stupid ones;
—still wear bathing suits, after three kids;
—levitate!
—consider myself a complete success only if one of my children or my pupils will grow up far better than I.

I can't:
—remember faces and names;
—prepare my own income tax returns;
—eat fast;
—eat soft pasty rice (yeeks!);
—laugh softly;
—sleep with the light on;
—keep my orchids and roses alive, even my bonsai which is supposed to thrive in the most adverse conditions;
—endure a shallow movie or book;
—revere authorities. I can only respect them;
—internalize what envy is. I can only admire—one of life's "rarest pleasures," says Ayn Rand.

I do:
—my TM and TM Sidhis twice a day, every day;
—read five hours each day;
—the best I can under any circumstances;
—return books that I borrow;
—value flexibility and its saving power;
—break rules which don't harmonize with good goals;
—overestimate people most of the time;
—revere the laws of nature whose workings I now have a clear idea of;
—attract dramatics in my life.

I don't:
—depend on anyone else for my happiness;
—care to please everybody;

140

—care to be liked by everyone;

—shortchange people at all;

—sell anyone, much less my friends or my principles for money,
   position or spite;

—watch TV;

—read newspapers anymore

—run away from my problems;

—believe in the impossible. If I did, I would not have had any single
   achievement at all;

—cry easily;

—forget bad turns so easily;

—snore;

—whisper;

—ever diet;

—abdicate my God-given ability to think and fend for myself.

That's me, in a pod!

WONDER KIDS? YEP!

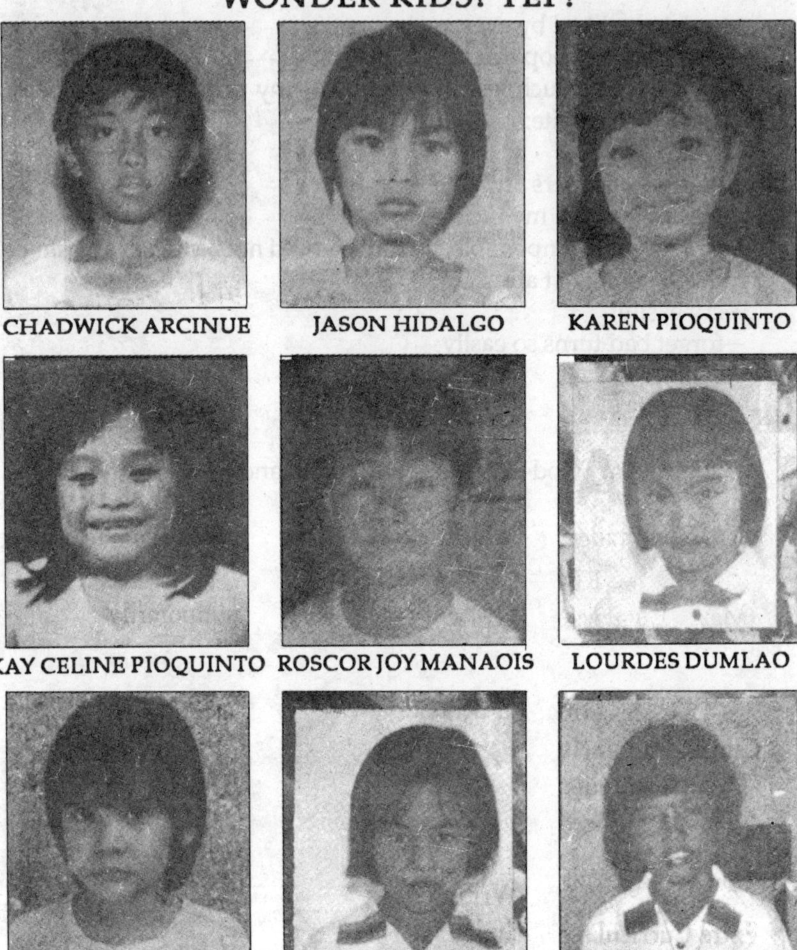

CHADWICK ARCINUE   JASON HIDALGO   KAREN PIOQUINTO

KAY CELINE PIOQUINTO   ROSCOR JOY MANAOIS   LOURDES DUMLAO

CHRISTINE MICHELLE SISON   JULITA FUERTES   MA. THERESA DISU

Because of Harvent Schools' non-graded approach to learning, these children finished the six-year elementary curriculum at age 9 and 10. Thereafter, Chad topped his entrance exams at the Ateneo de Manila and runs away with all the top academic awards each year; Jason is a star in the College of Journalism at UST; Karen and Kay are class valedictorians in high school; the rest are all scholars in a special Science High School.

Need we say more?

Bibliography

(The following books and periodicals were consulted either as source materials or for their ideas and theories.)

A. Books

Adams, Brian. *How to Succeed.*

Abrams, George J. *How I Made a Million Dollars with Ideas.* Chicago: Playboy Press, 1972.

Austen, Jane. *Emma.* New York: Dell Publishing Co., Inc., 1959.

Bailey, Herbert E. *The Essential Vitamin.* New York: Bantam Books, 1983.

Barrows, Sydney Biddle and William Novak. *Mayflower Madam.* New York: Ivy Books, 1986.

Bateson, Gregory. *Mind and Nature.* Toronto: Bantam Books, 1979.

Beecher, Willard and Marguerite. *Beyond Success and Failure.* New York: Pocket Books, 1966.

Bickel, Leonard. *Rise up to Life.* London: Angus and Robertson, 1972.

Bowen, Catherine Drinker. *Yankee from Olympus.* London: Ernest Benn Ltd., 1949.

Brown, Helen Gurley. *Having It All.* New York: Pocket Books, 1982.

Buck, Pearl S. *The Good Earth.* New York: Pocket Books, 1971.

Caldwell, Taylor. *Bright Flows the River.* New York: Doubleday and Co., 1978.

__________. *The Romance of Atlantis.* New York: Fawcett Books, 1975.

Chopra, Deepak. *Return of the Rishi.* Boston: Houghton Mifflin Co., 1988.

Clavell, James. *Noble House.* New York: Dell Publishing Co., Inc.1981.

__________. *Shogun.* New York: Dell Publishing Co., Inc., 1975.

__________. *Taipan.* New York: Dell Publishing Co., Inc., 1966.

Collier, Peter and David Horowitz. *The Rockefellers: An American Dynasty.* New York: Holt, Rinehart and Winston, 1976.

Cowan, Connell and Melvyn Kinder. *Smart Women, Foolish Choices.* New York: The New American Library, 1985.

Cunningham, Roger. *Curriculum Development in Nongraded Schools.* Goldnew Venture, 1971.

Daniken, Erich Von. *The Gold of the Gods.* New York: G.P. Putnam's Sons, 1973.

Dizon, Rolando R. (Ed.). *Educational Alternatives for the Future.* Quezon City: Phoenix Publishing House, 1983.

Doremus, Robert B. and Edgar W. Lacy, et al. *Patterns in Writing.* The Dryden Press, 1956.

Dostoyevsky, Fyodor. *The Brothers Karamazov.* New York: Dell Publishing Co., Inc. 1956.

Durant, Will and Ariel. *The Lessons of History.* New York: Simon & Schuster, 1968.

Dweck, Sylvia. *A Soul in Transit.* Manila: National Bookstore, Inc., 1986.

Edwards, Anne. *Road to Tara.* New York: Dell Publishing Co., Inc., 1983.

Egner, Robert E. (Ed.). *Bertrand Russell's Best.* London: George Allen & Unwin, Ltd., 1958.

Eliot, Charles W. (Ed.). *The Harvard Classics.* New York: P. F. Collier & Son Co., 1963.

Feldman, Anthony and Peter Ford. *Scientists and Inventors.* London: Aldus Books, 1979.

Frank, Philip. Einstein: *His Life and Times.* New York: A.A. Knopf, 1947.

Friedman, Milton and Rose. *Free to Choose.* New York: Avon Books, 1981.

Gann, Ernest K. *Masada.* New York: Jove Publications, Inc., 1970.

Gitelson, Bernard. *How to Make Your Own Luck.* New York: Warner Books, 1981.

Graham, Sheila. *How to Marry Super Rich or Love, Money and the Morning After.* New York: Grosset & Dunlap, 1974.

Green, Gerald. *Holocaust.* New York: Bantam Books, 1978.

Greene, Liz. *Relating.* Northamptonshire: The Aquarian Press, 1986.

Gunther, John. *Inside Russia Today.* New York: Harper & Bros., 1958.

Hadas, Moses (Ed.). *Greek Drama.* New York: Bantam Books. 1965.

Hailey, Elizabeth Forsythe. *A Woman of Independent Means.* New York: Avon Books, 1978.

Hainstock, Elizabeth G. *The Essential Montessori.* New York: Mentor Books, 1978.

Han Suyin. *The Enchantress.* New York: Bantam Books, 1985.

Hardy, Thomas. *The Return of the Native.* New York: The American Library of World Literature, Inc., 1959.

Hay, Julie and Charles E. Wingo. *Reading with Phonics.* Chicago: Lippincott Co., 1960.

Hesse, Hermann. *Siddhartha.* New York: New Directions Publishing Corporation, 1951.

Hill, Napoleon. *Grow Rich!—With Peace of Mind.* New York: Fawcett Crest. 1967.

Hillyer, V.M.*A Child's History of the World.* New York & London: The Century Co., 1924.

Holt, John. *Freedom and Beyond.* New York: E. P. Dutton Co., 1972.

Homer. *The Iliad.* New York: Walter J. Black, 1942.

__________. *The Odyssey.* New York: The New American Library, 1937.

Hurlock, Elizabeth B. *Guideposts for Growing Up.* Chicago: Standard Educational Corporation, 1979.

Hutchins, Robert Maynard (Ed.). *Masterpieces of Eloquence.* New York: Thomas Nelson and Sons, 1916.

Jaffe, Bernard. *Men of Science in America.* New York: Simon and Schuster, Inc., 1944.

Jaffe, Rona. *Class Reunion.* New York: Dell Publishing Co., Inc., 1979.

Jakes, John. *North and South.* New York: Dell Publishing Co., Inc., 1982.

James, Henry. *The Ambassadors.* New York: Dell Publishing Co., Inc., 1964.

Judd, H. Stanley. *Think Rich.* New York: Dell Publishing Co., Inc., 1978.

Kaddison, Ellis. *The Eighth Veil.* New York: Bantam Books, 1982.

Kane, Joseph Nathan. Facts about the Presidents. New York: Bantam Books, 1978.

Kaye, M.M. *The Far Pavilions.* New York: St. Martin's Press, 1978.

Kazantzakis, Nikos. *Zorba, the Greek.* London: Faber Ltd., 1961.

Kilduff, Marshall and Ron Javers. *Suicide Cult.* New York: Bantam Books, 1978.

Korda, Michael. *Success!* New York: Ballantine Books, 1977.

Khrishnamurti, J. *The Impossible Question.* Middlesex: Penguin Books, Ltd. 1978.

Laing, R. D. *The Politics of Experience.* New York: Ballantine Books, 1967.

Larrick, Nancy. *Encourage Your Child to Read.* New York: Dell Purse Books, 1980.

Lass, Abraham H. and Norma S. Tassman (Eds.). *Going to School.* New York: Mentor Books, 1980.

Lewis, Spencer H. *Cycles of Life.*: Supreme Grand Lodge of A.M.O.R.C., Inc., 1954.

Llewelyn, Richard. *How Green Was My Valley.* London: New English Library, Ltd., 1939.

McCarthy, Mary. *The Group.* New York: A Signet Book, 1964.

__________. *The Humanist in the Bathtub.* New York: Curtis Publishing Co., 1951.

McCullough, Colleen. *The Thorn Birds.* New York: Avon Books, 1977.

Mandino, Og (Ed.). *A Treasury of Success Unlimited.* New York: Pocket Books, 1978.

Michener, James A. *Texas.* New York: Fawcett Crest, 1985.

__________. *Hawaii.*

__________. *The Source.*

Mitchell, Margaret. *Gone with the Wind.* New York: Avon Books, 1973.

Montessori Maria. *The Absorbent Mind.* New York: Dell Publishing Co., Inc., 1967.

__________. *The Discovery of the Child.* Notre Dame, Indiana: Fides Publishers, Inc., 1967.

Naisbitt, John. *Megatrends.* New York: Warner Books, Inc., 1982.

Nouwen, Henri J.M. *Creative Ministry.* New York: Doubleday & Co., Inc., 1978.

O'Connell, John P. and Rex Martin (Eds.). *The Life of Christ.* Chicago: The Catholic Press, Inc., 1959.

Peter, Laurence J. and Raymond Hull. *The Peter Principle.* New York: William Morrow & Co., Inc., 1969.

Plain, Belva. *Evergreen.* New York: Dell Publishing Co., Inc., 1978.

Playfair, Guy I. and Scott Hill. *Cycles of Neaven.* New York: St. Martin's Press, 1978.

Quito, Emerita S. *Oriental Roots of Occidental Philosophy.* Manila: De la Salle University Press, 1975.

Rand, Ayn. *Anthem.* Caldwell, Idaho: The Caxton Printers, Ltd., 1946.

__________. *Atlas Shrugged.* New York: Random House, Inc., 1957.

__________. *The Fountainhead.* New York: A Signet Book, 1943.

__________. *The Virtue of Selfishness.* New York: A Signet Book, 1964.

__________. *We the Living.* New York: Random House, Inc., 1959.

Ringer, Robert J. *Looking Out for Number One.* New York: Fawcet Crest Books, 1977.

Romulo, Carlos P. *I Walked with Heroes.* New York: Holt, Rinehart & Winston, 1961.

Ropp, Robert S. de. *The Master Game.* New York: Dell Publishing Co., Inc., 1968.

Shah, Idries. *Thinkers of the East.* Suffolk: Richard Clay (Chaucer Press), Ltd., 1971.

Shakespeare, William. *Julius Caesar.* New York: Simon & Schuster, 1959.

Shaw, George Bernard. *Plays Extravagant.* Middlesex: Penguin Books, 1981.

Shaw, Irwin. *Rich Man, Poor Man.* New York: Dell Publishing Co., Inc., 1981.

Sheehy, Gail. *Passages.* New York: E. P. Dutton, 1976.

Singh, Hazur Maharaj Sawan Jr., *The Philosophy of the Masters.* Punjab, India, 1967.

Socrates, Jose B. (Ed.) *The Impact System of Mass Primary Education.* Quezon City: Innotech, 1983.

Sophocles. *Oedipus the King.* New York: Pocket Books, 1959.

Soriano, Liceria B. *Continuous Progression in Philippine Schools.* Quezon City: JMC Press, Inc., 1973.

Speare, Grace. *Everything Talks to Me.* New York: Berkeley Quicksilver Books, 1979.

Spiller, R. E. (Ed.). *Selected Essays, Lectures and Poems of Ralph Waldo Emerson.* New York: Pocket Books, 1985.

Stassinoupoulos, Arianne. Maria Callas: *The Woman behind the Legend*. New York: Ballantine Books, 1981.

Stone, Randolph. *The Mystic Bible*. Punjab, India: Radha Soami Satsang Beas, 1977.

Stowe, Harriet Beecher. *Uncle Tom's Cabin*. New York: Bantam Classic Edition, 1981.

Suzuki, Shunryu. *Zen Mind, Beginner's Mind* (Trudy Dixon, ed.). New York and Tokyo: , 1970.

Talbot, Michael. *Mysticism and the New Physics*. New York: Bantam Books, 1981.

Thompson, Jacqueline. *The Very Rich Book*. New York: William Morrow & Co., Inc., 1981.

Toffler, Alvin. *Future Shock*. New York: Bantam Books, 1970.

__________. *The Third Wave*. New York: Bantam Books, 1977.

Trahey, Jane. *On Women and Power*. New York: Avon Books, 1977.

Tolstoy, Leo. *War and Peace*. New York: Dell Publishing Co., Inc., 1955.

Uris, Leon. *QBVII*. New York: Bantam Books, 1970.

Vernon, P.E. (Ed.). *Creativity*. Suffolk, England. The Chaucer Press, 1973.

Virgil. *The Aeneid*. Middlesex, England: Penguin Books, 1956.

Wallace, Irving. *The Word*. New York: Pocket Books, 1972.

Walpole, Hugh. *Vanessa*. New York: The Sun Dial Press, Inc., 1937.

Whitehead, Alfred North. *The Aims of Education*. New York: The MacMillan Publishing Co., Inc., 1957.

Wiseman, Thomas. *The Money Motive*. London: , 1974.

Yogananda, Paramahansa. *Autobiography of a Yogi*. California: Self-Realization Fellowship, 1983.

__________. *They Changed Our World*. New York: Berkeley Books, 1982.

__________. *Heiress: The Rich Life of Marjorie Meriweather Post*. New York: New Republic Books, 1972.

__________. *Churchill Digest*. London: The Reader's Digest Associaton, Ltc., 1965.

__________. *Great Lives, Great Deeds*. London: The Reader's Digest Association, 1965.

__________. *Sayings of the Ayatollah Khomeini: Political, Philosophical, Social and Religious*. New York: Bantam Books, Inc., 1980.

__________. *What Has Religion Done for Mankind?* Brooklyn & New York: Watchtower Bible & Tract Society, Inc., 1951.

__________. *The Toynbee-Ikeda Debate*.

B. Periodicals

Bloom, Benjamin. "New Views of the Learner: Implications for Instruction and Curriculum." *Educational Leadership*, XXXV, No. 7 (April 1978), pp. 563-576.

Callwood, June. "The One Sure Way to Happiness." *The Reader's Digest.* November 1974, pp. 109-112.

Case, Anna Lou. "Promoting Written Expression among Children," *The Educational Digest*, Vol. XXXIV, No. 7 (March 1974), pp. 46-47.

De Guzman, Flora. "Making Money," *Women's Journal,* Vol. XIII, No. 16 (July 6, 1985), pp. 32-33.

Dizon, Paulo D. "Not Enough Fuel in the World," *Philippine Literature in English.* Baguio City: St. Louis University, 1970.

Duggan, John M. "Dedication Address," *The Courier* (Winter 1983), Indiana: St. Mary's College.

Eastman, Max. "What Plato Says to Us," *The Reader's Digest* (September 1961), pp. 140-144.

Fischer, John. "Is There a Teacher in the Faculty?" *Harper's Magazine* (February 1965).

__________. "Cheers for Old Curmudgeon!" *The Reader's Digest* (October 1970), pp. 42-44.

Gardner, John W. "Know Yourself." *The Reader's Digest* (December 1963).

Gordon, Arthur. "Dan Fader's Help Yourself Textbooks," *American Education* (September 1967).

Hansen, Merell J. "Understanding Youth. It's Tough Growing Up but We Can Help," *Educational Leadership*, Vol. XXXV, No. 7 (April 1978), pp. 534-540.

Highet, Gilbert. "The Pleasures of Learning," *The Reader's Digest* (January 1977), pp. 105-108.

__________. "The Immortal Profession," *The Reader's Digest* (January 1977).

Hope, Bob. "The Importance of Having Fun," *The Reader's Digest* (February 1972), pp. 125-128.

Joly, Roxee W. "Schools in the People's Republic of China," *The Educational Digest,* Vol. XXXIX, No. 7 (March 1974), pp. 2-6.

Lagemann, John Kord. "Can We Make Human Beings More Intelligent?" *The Reader's Digest* (June 1966), pp. 77-81.

Maynard, Fredelle B. "The Teacher Gap and How to Close It," *The Reader's Digest*

Ross, Murray G. "How Can Universities Cope with Change?" *The Globe Magazine* (November 14, 1970).

Rummel, Frances V. "He Teaches Kids to Teach Themselves," *PTA Magazine* (October 1965).

Schiller, Ronald. "Bill Lear: Inventor of the 'Impossible,'" *The Reader's Digest* (September 1971), pp. 120-124.

Selwynn, Amy. "No More Homework?" *This Week Magazine* (May 13,   1951).

Shultz, Gladys Denny. "Is This the School of Tomorrow?" *Better Homes and Gardens* (September 1945).

Smith, Keith. "Good Schools, Bad Schools . . ." *The Reader's Digest* (June 1975), pp. 69-72.

Stewart, Gordon James. "Dr. Seuss: Fanciful Sage of Childhood," *The Reader's Digest* (August 1964), pp. 40-44.

___________ . "How to Be a Millionaire by 40," *Time* (December 3, 1965).

___________ . "Danger Signals in the Seven Ages of Man," *Women's Journal* (September 15, 1985).

___________ . "Mikimoto, Cultured Pearls Farmed in Japan," *Guarantee*, No. HB 127 (September 16, 1960).

___________ . "Catholic Schools and Quality Education," *Women's Word* (July 1982), pp. 30-34 & 40.

From the Grolier Information Service, Danbury, Connecticut, I found the following reports indispensable:

Pierre Teilhard de Chardin
The Underachiever
Recent Trends in Education
Evaluating and Reporting Pupil Progress
Individualized Instruction in the Elementary School
The Non-Graded School
Programmed Instruction
Criteria for Evaluating Schools
Children's Fears
Bureaucracy
Motivation in the Classroom
The Psychology of Fear
Self-Concept
Realism As a Philosophy of Education
Conducting Group Discussions
The Year-Round School
Pragmatism As a Philosophy of Education
Albert Einstein
Einstein's Theory of Relativity
Einstein's Unified Field Theory
Thomas Alva Edison
The World of the Future
Maria Montessori and the Montessori Method
The Slow Learner
Jean Piaget
Hints for Passing Examinations
Science Education in the Elementary Grades